ANCIENT SCOTLAND

A Guide to the Remains

Lloyd Laing

DAVID & CHARLES
NEWTON ABBOT   LONDON
NORTH POMFRET (VT)   VANCOUVER

ISBN 0 7153 7243 2
Library of Congress Catalog Card Number 76–11961

Set in 11 on 13pt Centaur
and printed in Great Britain
by Latimer Trend & Company Ltd Plymouth
for David & Charles (Publishers) Limited
Brunel House   Newton Abbot   Devon

Published in the United States of America
by David & Charles Inc
North Pomfret   Vermont 05053   USA

Published in Canada
by Douglas David & Charles Limited
1875 Welch Street   North Vancouver   BC

CONTENTS

LIST OF ILLUSTRATIONS

List of Illustrations

PREFACE

The ancient remains of Scotland chronicle her 6,000 years of turbulent history. But, more than this, they tell of the things that history ignores; the life and environment of the people, from the rich to the poor, warrior to peasant, hunter to goldsmith. From the great tower houses and palaces of the sixteenth century to the unpretentious silver brooches and simple stone huts of the ten centuries before, the remains leave something for all tastes. They can be found in the heart of the great cities, in pretty villages, or after long trudges across bleak moorland.

Here is a selection of the most readily visible remains both in museums and on the ground that may help Scotland's admirers to enjoy the past around them.

I

THE FIRST ADVENTURERS

To the Roman soldiers from Syria or Spain, few landscapes could have seemed as uninviting as the cold wet forests of Caledonia. Policing the most northerly frontier in the Empire was a struggle against the elements as well as the hostile barbarians who continually harassed the civilised world. For decades the effective end of civilisation ran abruptly from the Forth to the Clyde—through the industrial heart of modern Scotland.

But there were men, 6,000 years before the Romans, for whom the same land was the real end of the world. The ice sheet, which now bars humans from living near the North Pole, had stretched as far south as London. It was not until this frozen frontier melted and moved northwards that the land that became Scotland was uncovered. Eventually, south of the ice sheet grew up a vast dark forest in which roamed elk and deer, bear and wolf. Attracted by the new sources of food came the most rugged and adventurous of the human race. They pitted their brain and their brawn against the elements and began the struggle between man and the environment in Scotland.

The struggle left no violent marks on the landscape—no structures as impressive as the castles and palaces, stately homes and works of art which ensure that later Scotsmen have not been forgotten. Every now and then, insignificant-looking pieces of bone or stone are washed out of the soil of an Edinburgh park, the gentle fields near Roxburgh, or the caves near Oban to remind us of the debt modern Scotland owes to the first Mesolithic hunters who opened up the area. The stones and bones that find their way into museums for cataloguing or analysis are often barely distinguishable from works of nature to the casual observer, but

9

with them animals were hunted, killed and skinned and most of the necessities of life, such as tents, clothes and tools, made. Along the shores where today determined men prospect for oil, in 4000 BC, people hacked and scraped limpets off the rocks with an even greater urgency. Human beings started the chain of events that has led to the building of the rocket bases in the Hebrides and the oil rigs off the Shetlands.

As people toiled and died on Atlantic shores, in more favourable climates others had discovered the advantages of farming. When plants are tended and animals are herded it is possible to build up food stores and at last win the battle against nature. It was no longer necessary to depend entirely on the fickleness of the climate or the migrations of wild animals. If the animals moved north, humans no longer needed to follow, taking their few belongings and their tents. The future was assured in a store of golden grain and herds of pigs, sheep and goats. More permanent and comfortable dwellings could be built. Where there was stability there was time for thought and invention. People could contemplate their gods, and fill their surplus hours making functional objects attractive and irksome chores easier.

The idea of farming came to Scotland between 4000 and 3000 BC and the forests, already partly felled, were attacked by more modern, polished, stone axes. The countryside around Moray and Banff in particular became scattered with ranches and farmsteads. Peacefully grazing herds of small but sturdy animals enclosed in kraals would have greeted the eye of the traveller in Neolithic Scotland. Beyond the cattle enclosures were fields of grain crops that bordered the remaining forests. While some men tilled the fields and tended the herds, others would have continued to venture after the game as their fathers and grand-fathers had done before them, or to push their hollowed, oak canoes onto the treacherous waters to catch the silver harvest of sea and river. The edge of the world had been conquered at last.

In these remote days men were few in a vast world. It is unlikely that more than a few thousand people lived in the whole of Scotland during the Neolithic Age. Near neighbours would have been rare and aggression confined to family squabbles. Yet these were not 'noble savages' living in some Golden Age before the Fall. The assets of a settled life were matched by the ills. Disease would have spread more rapidly, and genetic weaknesses would have been transmitted more frequently now that not only the fittest could survive. Home-produced crops were not reliable—a crop failure or animal disease could result in malnutrition or death as surely as the perils of nomadic life. The addition of cereal to the diet led to a rapid increase of dental caries—many a Neolithic farmer must have lain awake in his wooden hut nursing toothache.

VISIBLE REMAINS

Of the Mesolithic hunters no settlements or buildings survive for the visitor to look at. A camp was excavated at Morton (Fife) and several caves near Oban are known to have been occupied. Mesolithic remains are best seen in the display cases of museums.

From Neolithic times—the period of the farming communities—remains are more extensive. Monumental tombs, some house sites and many objects in museums can be seen.

NEOLITHIC TOMBS

It sometimes happens that because a society lavished great attention on its funerary monuments we know more about its way of death than its way of life. Because virtually all the visible remains consist of earthen burial mounds, many with dank, stone-built passages and chambers, the Neolithic period tends to be associated with ritual and superstition. It is highly probable that Neolithic belief did involve a great deal that would be unpalatable if not horrific to civilised twentieth-century minds, but it is improbable that the first farmers were as totally obsessed with death as they appear from archaeological remains. Indeed the chambered tombs that are so impressive today were the last resting places of the élite—the majority of the population were almost certainly interred without undue ceremony in simple underground graves that have rarely come to light. Many Neolithic tombs lie in remote areas where they have escaped the onslaught of bulldozers or stone robbers. In the half-light of early morning or late evening, it is easy for even the most down-to-earth traveller to imagine the wild rituals that were performed around them—rituals that resulted in the large-scale smashing of pottery, the scattering of charred bones, the blocking of the main entrances and the interment of dog skulls with those of men.

There are two types of Neolithic tomb in Scotland, longbarrows and chambered tombs.

Longbarrows

These are usually trapezoidal mounds of earth or stone which frequently cover timber structures called mortuary houses. The remains of mortuary houses were found in excavation under mounds at Lochhill (Kirkcudbright) and Daladies (Kincardine). The tombs were the equivalent of family vaults and were the efforts of a single community.

Chambered Tombs

These are more numerous and impressive than longbarrows. Current estimates suggest that these stone-built mounds, with their internal passages and chambers for the burial of the dead, were built over a period of twenty-two centuries—longer than Christianity has yet lasted. Many were added to or modified and the result is a perplexing variety that taxes the ingenuity of scholars attempting their classification.

Nowhere in Scotland have the Neolithic people left so many funereal remains than on the Orkadian island of Rousay. Like bosses on a shield they are spread out around the coast in the tufted heather. They are now covered with turfed-over concrete domes that enable the visitor to enter the chambers safely and inspect them in the cold dim glow afforded by skylights. Each one is different, ranging from the minute example, too small to enter, that lies beside the unique two-storied Taversoe Tuick, to the vast multi-chambered Midhowe, too extensive to roof with concrete. Instead the visitor to Midhowe inspects the fungus-stained remains from catwalks under a monstrous barn-like construction.

Of the tombs on the mainland, none are more impressive than the two Grey Cairns of Camster, on a bleak moor in Caithness. Camster Long is an outstanding example of a multi-period construction. The long cairn of stones which is visible today was built over two smaller tombs, the

Fig 1   Reconstruction of Mid Gleniron chambered tomb soon after completion, Wigtownshire

earlier of which had an unusual polygonal chamber. In the second tomb a passage led to a chamber of stone slabs that formed 'stalls' or segments in which burials would have been laid. The enclosing cairn was faced with a double wall and terminated at both ends in horns that form courtyards. It was perhaps in these courtyards that funeral rituals were held. An idea of the original appearance of individual tombs can be gained from the adjacent Camster Round, where the intrepid can crawl down a passageway into the heart of the mound, eerily lit by a skylight.

Unintentionally, by the very construction of the tombs, the builders left modern man clues to the world they lived in. Because Rousay has been sparsely populated, we can be fairly certain that nearly all the prehistoric tombs that were built have survived the hand of time. Each tomb is built on a separate unit of land and apparently served a population of between twenty and thirty people at any one time. The construction of long barrows such as Daladies probably involved several thousand man hours, while some of the chambered tombs must have taken as much as 7,000 hours to construct. This implies that each group had help from its neighbours. From this we can infer that already by 3000 BC there was some kind of clan organisation in Scotland.

It is impossible to tell whether each tomb was the conception of one or several individuals. Maes Howe in Orkney, at least, must have been the brilliant conception of a single architect. Without visiting the monuments it is difficult to appreciate the immense task involved in their erection. No metal tools were used and stone blocks, often weighing several tons, were hoisted into position with mechanical aids no more complicated than wedges, rollers, or levers. These erections were being put up almost a thousand years before the pyramids in Egypt, and without the benefits of a civilised society.

Houses

In the winter of 1850 a bad storm blew up on the western mainland of Orkney and as usual the inhabitants settled down to wait until the worst was over, for storms are a normal feature of life in these exposed islands looking out across the Atlantic to North America. This storm, however, was unusually severe. As it raged across the Bay of Skaill it stripped the grass from the sand dunes, whirling up the sand of one particular dune, known locally as Skara Brae, to lay bare the stone walls of ancient dwellings.

The laird of Skaill, William Watt, went out to inspect the damage and, being of an antiquarian turn of mind, began to explore the mound. By 1868 he had cleared four huts of their filling and revealed part of the dwelling of a community that had ended as dramatically as Roman Pompeii. Despite the amazing antiquity of the dwellings, it was not until 1925, when another storm damaged the cleared huts and midden, that the site came once more to the forefront of scholars' attention. A seawall was built, and the greatest prehistorian of the day, Gordon Childe, was called in to excavate the site scientifically, in advance of consolidation. So remarkable were the finds that even Professor Childe could not believe they were more than about 1,400 years old.

Another find at Rinyo, a similar but less well preserved village on Rousay, provided a vital clue. A sherd of pottery from here was identical to others found in British sites known from other evidence to have been occupied in the early second millennium BC. The village of Skara Brae was thus proved to have flourished during the Neolithic period. To this day the village remains the best preserved settlement of the period in Europe. The feature that ensured that Skara Brae survived, where most settlements of the period have left few discernible traces except in excavation, is that the shortage of wood in the northern isles forced the

Fig 2 Reconstruction of a hut interior at Skara Brae, Orkney

inhabitants to build everything of stone. The houses survive almost to roof level and each room, about 15–20ft (4·5–6·1m) square, contains stone furniture, as though it were a megalithic shop showroom. In the centre are stone hearths for peat-burning, and stone-slab dressers stand against the walls. To the sides are low stone boxes which were probably made more comfortable with skins and furs and used as beds. Clay-lined boxes were set in the floor and probably used to store food. Meals seem to have consisted of shellfish, mutton, beef and barley. Everyday tools were simple and pottery was crude.

burghshire, Selkirkshire, Stirlingshire, Ayrshire and Argyll. Welsh axe-factory products have been found in West Lothian. Scotland too had sources of suitable stone, and a flourishing trade developed in Arran pitchstone, which was exported particularly to south-east Scotland, but which reached Wigtownshire and north-east England. Rhum bloodstone was exported, and Shetland developed its own trade in Riebeckite. From further afield still came polished axes of jadeite, ceremonial objects too delicate to use. The type of stone from which they were produced probably came to southern Scotland from the German Rhineland.

Axes were not the only stone tools. Flint, the material favoured in England, is rare in Scotland, and though some was imported, other stones that could fracture to a sharp edge were used, such as chert. Difficult materials were often fashioned into neat leaf-shaped arrowheads and flint knives and all-purpose tools called scrapers were made. Stone was also used for making mace-heads at a time when metal was making its first appearance in Scotland—the inspiration was probably the traditional antler mattocks, but battle-axes brought in by metal-using incomers served as the immediate models. Jet was used for sliders (probably belt fasteners), and bone for a variety of objects such as pins, particularly in the Northern Isles.

It is, however, their pottery that is the most distinctive product of the agriculturalists, and by studying the different forms and where these were found, archaeologists have been able to trace the spread and development of farming communities. The earliest pots were plain, bag-shaped vessels, without decoration and probably intended as imitations of leather receptacles. The most distinctive have a graceful shoulder and a rim, outbent to stop a string slipping off. Later pots were richly decorated, sometimes with incised linear patterns, sometimes with the impression of twisted cords perhaps intended to imitate basketry.

Very little that can be termed art survives from this period in Scotland. There are, however, some mysterious linear patterns cut into the stones of Skara Brae that look, almost certainly fortuitously, like a primitive form of writing, and there are also eyebrow and eye patterns carved on the stones of the chambered tomb of the Holm of Papa Westray in Orkney, perhaps intended as a representation of a deity presiding over the tomb. Some of the pottery used by the Skara Brae people displays more ambitious art—one sherd has an elaborate pattern of a spiral and lozenges, while others from the similar but less well preserved village of Rinyo have triangular and lozenge patterns. Spiral patterns also adorn a strange series of carved stone balls peculiar to Scotland, most of which if not all are probably from this time—one was found at Skara Brae. They could have been used for almost anything—in a game perhaps, or as bolas for bringing down animals.

2

HEROES AND GOLDSMITHS

Cairnpapple hill is one of the most extraordinary prehistoric monuments in Scotland. Situated on a hill which commands a wide view of the surrounding countryside to the silvery waters of the Forth, six miles away, the slight remains of a mound and ditch, and some holes in the ground, chronicle a thousand years of primitive religion. The hill was first selected for religious observance by the Neolithic farmers who began practising their new rituals. The oak and hazel were cleared from the summit, with axes made in the Lake District and North Wales, to form a simple sacred area. Three huge stones dominated an arc of cremation burials. After a few centuries the plan was rethought, the stones wrested from their sockets and the entire area enclosed by a ditch hewn from the living rock. Worshippers arriving through one of the two entrances would have been confronted with an oval circle of twenty-six standing stones, like jagged giant's teeth.

Time passed, and new generations brought changes to the summit. More imposing cenotaphs became fashionable. Just as the introduction of farming had heralded new religious manners, the times were being dominated by the use of a new material—metal. As if to impress in the minds of the population the importance of the modern ways of thinking, a massive cairn, 50ft (12·2m) in diameter, was thrown up over burials. Eventually the cairn was doubled in size, and burials set within it. The mound sprawled across several of the sockets of the old stone circle and part of the silted-up ditch. The old ideas of the Neolithic period were being symbolically replaced by the new. The age of bronze had arrived in Scotland.

THE BRONZE AGE

The Bronze Age was a time that abounded with new ideas and inventions. Coinciding with the elaboration of the henge at Cairnpapple, a new way of life, at least for the upper levels of society, grew up. The objects placed in graves from this time onward suggest that wealth was equated with power, power with war and war with weaponry. The rich graves of the early Bronze Age with their occasional glint of gold speak

Fig 3   Reconstruction of Cairnpapple Hill, West Lothian, at the beginning of the Bronze Age, *c* 1800 BC

silently of heroes and warriors whose exploits might have been similar to those recounted by Homer. The tomb at the Knowes of Trotty (Orkney) with its resplendent gold 'sun disc' might well have been the last resting place of a British Ajax. The warrior chiefs who presided over the population of farmers and hunters owed their ascendancy primarily to the use of copper. The art of working this metal reached Britain

21

about 2500 BC and within 500 years people in Scotland were adding tin to form the infinitely more useful alloy, bronze.

The advent of metal technology opened up a new chapter in the social evolution of early Scotland. New trades and occupations were demanded. Until this time only a few men followed specialised occupations (such as the production of stone implements), but now skilled workers were required for the smelting, casting and prospecting of ores. Suddenly new areas became vital—good agricultural land was no longer the most valuable commodity. The whereabouts of copper and tin ores became important knowledge. Such areas were few and far between and people travelled further and more frequently than ever before since their ancestors followed the deer in the wake of the ice sheet. Trade became more important and areas with copious ores near the surface became powerful and rich. Opportunists were quick to direct the efforts of the craftsmen who beat the gold and forged the bronze. Naturally such specialisation and riches led to rivalries between individuals and larger groups. The warrior fought not only for personal glory, but for the riches of gold.

VISIBLE REMAINS

Some of the visible remains of the Bronze Age are among the most inpressive in Scottish prehistory. The henge monuments, massive standing stones, burial cairns and other funerary monuments are most common, though in a few places slight and uninspiring remains of the homes and fields of the early metal users can be seen.

Henge Monuments

At about the time when the Bronze-Age ways of life were developing, the henge monuments in Britain were becoming more elaborate, furnished (as was Cairnpapple, p 20) with two opposed entrances instead of one, and often with rings of standing stones. The Ring of Brodgar and the Stenness Stones (Orkney) rival even Cairnpapple in scenic beauty, and in contrast have many of their original stones preserved *in situ.*

The Stones of Stenness and the Ring of Brodgar stand on opposite sides of the narrow isthmus of land which separates Loch Harray from Loch Stenness on the Orkney mainland and across which a processional avenue of stones once stretched. Attendant on them is a rash of small burial mounds which cluster in their shadow like officiating priests. Within sight of the whole complex squats the huge mound of Maes Howe, a benign patriarch among his younger flock. On summer evenings under the low northern sun, the few indications of the presence of modern man fade into insignificance. The only evidence of life comes from the cries of birds rising off the gleaming waters of the lochs, and little has changed since men honoured their beliefs here 4,000 years ago.

The Brodgar circle encloses an area 360ft (109·7m) in diameter. The largest of the twenty-seven surviving stones towers 15ft (4·5m) high, while one of the Stenness circle stones achieves 17ft (5·2m). The Stones of Stenness were recently excavated when a trilithon setting of stones was knocked down by vandals, and the excavation showed that originally there had been twelve stones set out with geometrical accuracy round the inside of a ditch over 12ft (3·6m) wide and 7ft (2·1m) deep. The excavators found that the vandalised stones had been set up entirely through Victorian fancy, inspired by Sir Walter Scott. Originally, in the centre of the circle, a square setting of four stones with cremated bones and fragments of pottery had stood next to a series of mysterious pits containing pottery, charred grain and a fragment of a stone implement.

Stone Circles

Stone circles can also be found without the encircling ditches of henges. Of these, the most spectacular is Callanish (Lewis), set in a windswept Atlantic landscape. But Callanish is no simple circle of standing stones. Two giant avenues converge from nowhere on a circular monument. Two burial cairns, like balls in a giant fossilised game of roulette, lie in the centre of the sacred area, while attendant cairns and stones watch from the heather.

Less monumental versions of the basic stone circle are found in many parts of Scotland. Good examples can be seen, for instance, at Torhouse (Wigtownshire) or Lamlash (Arran).

At Temple Wood, Kilmartin (Argyll), a circle of stones encloses a massive cist, now without its burial. In this example, however, the stones are probably all that remain of a kerb round a very large cairn which has long since been robbed away. It is a useful reminder that pre-historic monuments have often had a chequered career; cairns covering burials were often robbed of their stone, leaving only the massive stones of the burial chamber open to the sky, while in other cases farmers or antiquaries have added structures (as at Stenness) which they felt *should* have been there.

Of all the prehistoric monuments of Scotland, few have attracted more legends than stone circles. As in England, stories of people being turned to stone, of hauntings, or of the stones rising up to drink at nearby streams or shores are widespread. One Perthshire circle now has trees growing in the place of vanished stones, and a curse is said to fall on anyone who attempts to break the circle. When the owner, con-temptuous of tradition, began to cut down one of the trees a few years ago, the saw slipped, badly wounding him. The tree still stands, the circle complete.

Ring Cairns

Widespread in northern Britain are funerary monuments usually called ring cairns—low mounds of stones set in a circle in which burials were laid, the cairns frequently being demarcated by a kerb of larger stones.

The earliest and most distinctive ring cairns in Scotland are recumbent stone circles, so called because a large slab was placed horizontally be-tween two flanking uprights at some point in the circumference, with a burial cairn in the centre. These are to be found concentrated in the north-east, and good examples can be seen at Loanhead of Daviot, East Aquhorthies and Tomnaverie (Aberdeenshire).

A related type of monument, the Clava cairn, to be seen in Inverness-shire, may be the prototype for the series. It is really no more than an unusual type of chambered tomb with a circular chamber approached by a long passage through the cairn. In contrast to the earlier chambered tombs, the Clava cairns seem to have been the tombs of only one, perhaps two, cremated individuals.

Stone Circles and Astronomy

Much debate has surrounded the astronomical function of henges and stone circles, and claims have sometimes been made that monuments such as Stonehenge are giant computers or lunar observatories. As with many of the wilder claims that beset the fringes of archaeology, until recently such ideas were unsupported by any real evidence, but in 1967 Alexander Thom, emeritus Professor of Engineering at Oxford, published a report on stone circles in all parts of Britain, of which he had accurately surveyed over 500. From this survey, and work done subsequently, it is now possible to make a number of fairly sound deductions about prehistoric British mathematics.

By no means are all the apparent circles truly circular. Some are egg-shaped, others laid out with circles of different diameters superimposed. Even more remarkable are those having ellipses with two foci, which shows a knowledge of conic sections comparable to that of the civilised Greeks a thousand years later. Pythagoras, too, was anticipated in the laying out of some circles. Throughout, a basic unit of 2·72ft seems to have been used—now popularly called the 'megalithic yard'. The same measurement was used all over Britain, and shows not even slight local variation, suggesting that some measure of control ensured uniformity.

Whether the stone circles served as astronomical observatories is another matter. There can be little doubt that some of the greater monuments, such as Stonehenge and possibly Callanish (Lewis), were used to trace the movements of the sun and moon and possibly the rising and setting of a few stars, such as Capella. A few sites probably had alignments to represent a sixteen-month year by dividing the horizon between the solstitial sunrises, while other sites may have marked the four extremes of moonrise and moonset. All this suggests that there was an accumulation of traditional knowledge handed down, perhaps among a 'priesthood' who knew about basic geometry and how to lay out the circles. This does not, of course, mean that the builders of Callanish were outstanding astronomers or mathematical geniuses. Their interest was probably practical and concerned with the effect of the changing seasons on the farming calendar. Many of the small circles are not entirely astronomical, and appear to have been primarily burial sites, though sometimes an orientation on the rising sun is detectable.

Burials

The numerous crumbling urns and oxidised bronzes that survive from bronze-using Scotland shed interesting light on the world of Bronze-Age man. In the early part of the period, the dead were inhumed, often with splendidly decorated beakers (probably beer mugs). Pottery making had improved enormously and the vessels were prized. As time progressed, the more up to the minute Bronze-Age people favoured few grave goods and cremation.

Bronze-Age people built their funerary monuments on a scale not contemplated in Britain before or since. At Kilmartin (Argyll) the finest complex of burial sites of the time in Scotland, can be seen. A linear cemetery stretches over three miles. The earliest is a Neolithic chambered tomb called Nether Largie South, which was followed by six others containing stone coffins. Linear cemeteries are common not in Scotland, but in the great Bronze-Age culture of Wessex. This warrior society produced Stonehenge, and had connections with the civilisations of the eastern Mediterranean. Several of the coffins in the Kilmartin cairns are composed of carefully dressed slabs which have been grooved or chamfered to slot into one another, as in woodworking. This technique recalls the tenon and mortise jointing of Stonehenge, and is a copy of a wooden-coffin construction. Carvings of flat bronze axes on some of the coffin slabs, namely in the Ri Cruin cairn and the north cairn of Nether Largie, are found elsewhere only on the trilithons of Stonehenge. A grooved cist slab from nearby Badden had a pattern of multiple lozenges which were similar to the gold multiple lozenges found in a rich Wessex burial at Bush Barrow (Wiltshire). From such connections as these we can infer close links between Wessex and Argyll.

Cup and Ring Marks

The purpose of cup and ring marks, which are found widely in northern Britain, is unknown. They could be prospectors' signs, or, more probably, connected with religious ritual. Although a variety of patterns, including sun symbols, axes and footprints are found, the majority of cup-and-ring-carved stones simply have hollows or 'cups' pecked into the rock, often with one or more circles round them. A few of the more ornate carvings on cists may be intended to represent everyday objects hanging on the wall of the house of the dead. There are good collections at Kilmichael Glassary, Carnbaan, Balucraig, Achnabreck and Ballygowan (Argyll) and on rock outcrops at Drumtroddan (Wigtownshire).

Houses and Fields

One of the very few British houses excavated from the beginning of the metal-using period is at Northton, on the south-west tip of Harris (Hebrides). The site was intermittently occupied from the Stone Age until the Middle Ages. Two drystone houses from the early Bronze Age seem to have been little more than revetted hollows in the sand, protected by a roof of animal skins supported on flimsy stakes. The better preserved house was 28ft (8·5m) long and 14ft (4·3m) wide, with a hearth in the middle of the floor. The middens, a good reflection of the diet, consisted mainly of the bones of sheep, cattle and red deer.

Settlement sites in the later part of the epoch have left as few visible remains. From excavation it appears that most of the Lowlands were scattered with palisaded, round, timber huts. In the north, where wood was scarce, round stone-built huts known as 'courtyard houses' were furnished (like their Neolithic precursors in Orkney) with stone fittings.

A few field systems of the later Bronze Age have recently been recognised. The predominant type consists of small irregular fields formed by banks, scattered with piles of stones gathered in field clearance and often associated with timber buildings or hut circles. Towards the end of the Bronze Age, however, the climate deteriorated badly, and the population seems to have given up crops in favour of animal husbandry in many areas.

EVERYDAY LIFE

The people in the Bronze Age led diverse lives, according to their callings. The standard of workmanship of the many objects produced at the time was a considerable improvement on the preceding age. Superb pottery beakers, decorated simply but tastefully with the impressions of twisted cords adorned many a chieftain's feast. Such beakers went out of fashion to be replaced by what the Victorians called, unimaginatively, 'food vessels'. By the end of the Bronze Age the most popular pots were less aesthetically pleasing—plain vessels with flat rims, reminiscent of buckets, and potters were kept busy making pottery cinerary urns.

It was the goldsmith's art that grew to ascendancy in this period. The rich warriors wore gold necklets (*lunulae*), no doubt as status symbols, and later commissioned penannular armlets and dress fasteners. Their hair was adorned with sheet-gold penannular trinkets, while fine sundiscs (circular gold plates with no known function unless for decoration) and lock rings distinguished the élite from the mass of the population. Even functional objects, such as the socket of a spearhead in a hoard from Pyotdykes (Angus), were decorated with the incorruptible metal.

Whatever the merits of gold, however, it cannot be used for weapons or tools. The warriors depended on their strength for their power, so it was copper and later bronze that was worked in most profusion. Simple flat copper axes and daggers were used first. A warrior burial at Ashgrove (Fife) was afforded the last rites of an unknown barbarian ritual. The body was covered with a mass of leaves—a surgical dressing might have been the function of some sphagnum moss, and lime and meadow sweet an offering from a grieving relative. But in addition to these offerings there was a more positive tribute to the warrior himself—a dagger hilt, with two horn hiltplates fixed in place with bronze rivets and an ivory pommel.

Copper and bronze weapons were probably used in battle, but it is less certain whether the bronze shields that are sometimes found in Scotland ever had to withstand sword cut or spear thrust. When experiments were made with replicas of bronze shields of the period it was found that they were useless against a serious attack with genuine Bronze-Age weapons. More effective in protecting the body was a leather shield, made to the specifications of a surviving example from an Irish peatbog. This sustained only slight scratches after repeated bombardment by the sword.

It is highly probable, therefore, that the bronze shields were used in ritual and ceremonial rather than in battle. The Bronze Age was a time when outward ostentation was important and people could afford such leisurely extravagances as symbols of prestige and status.

The climax to the Bronze Age came around 1000 BC, when a wide range of objects, from the purely ceremonial to the functional, were produced.

How were these objects made? Open stone moulds were first used for casting simple objects such as flat axes, tanged, flat knives and awls. Eventually, however, smiths developed the use of a two-piece mould and of *ciré perdue* (lost-wax casting). The latter involved making a wax model of the object, building up a clay mould around it and then melting the wax leaving a perfect mould for the metal. Relatively complex castings were thus possible.

One of the difficulties Bronze-Age man encountered was in keeping the bronze part of his weapons and tools attached to their wooden handles. His inventive powers were sorely tried. Flat axes were given up in favour of those first with hammered and then cast flanges which prevented the blade from wobbling. Later a stop ridge was added to prevent the blade splitting the haft on impact. In further developments still the flanges were bent over to form a socket until by the end of the period true socketed axes were being cast.

A wide variety of small tools from the numerous founders' hoards can be seen in museums, notably in the National Museum of Antiquities in Edinburgh, including socketed gouges, razors and sickles. Bronze armlets were made as personal adornment, and beaten bronze used to cover jet buttons.

In spheres outside warfare the metal-users still resorted to stone on occasions. Elaborate necklaces dating from the middle of the era were strung together with spacer plates dividing barrel-shaped jet beads. A glassy substance called faience was sometimes worn as beads. Although this was popular around the Mediterranean, and probably imported, some opinion holds it to be of local Scottish manufacture. Bone was used for making toggles for skin clothing and for beads.

Good collections of Bronze-Age objects can be seen in several museums in Scotland, and many smaller local museums often have a few exhibits of this period. The best displays can be seen in the National Museum in Edinburgh, the Kelvingrove and Hunterian Museums in Glasgow, Dundee Museum and Dumfries Burgh Museum.

3

THE MEN OF IRON

On a remote island off the coast of Shetland stands a gaunt tower. The island is now totally uninhabited, except by sheep and the seabirds that rise up in a dark cloud at dusk from the parapet at the top. The Broch of Mousa, which looks like the cooling tower of some impossible prehistoric steelworks, has been protected for sixteen hundred years from the ravages of man by its isolation.

Compare this early Iron-Age edifice with the stone circles, chambered tombs or tiny stone huts of the preceding epoch and even the most casual visitor can observe that great steps had been taken between the building of these and the construction of Mousa. What then happened between the Bronze Age and the first century AD to produce such a change in building techniques and social structure? The answer is to be found in the arrival of the Celts.

THE COMING OF THE CELTS

The philosopher Aristotle wrote: 'We have no word for the man who is extremely fearless, perhaps he may be termed mad or without feeling, who is not afraid of either earthquake or waves, as they say of the Celts.' This is a rare instance of a Greek being at a loss for a word. Celtic bravery was renowned amongst their enemies, the Romans; and the strong warrior-based society suggested by written accounts, is backed up by archaeological finds.

The story of the Celts is as chaotic and diverse as the barbarians were themselves. From the time they first set foot on British shores, in the seventh century BC, they had an important impact on the population.

Celtic society, enriched by profits from salt and iron, had developed on the Continent where a loose frontier was held against the nomads of the Steppes. From these fierce fighters the Celts learned to ride horses, to use iron and to fashion it into short swords. These arts the Celts transmitted to Britain. The Celticisation of Scotland was gradual and subtle —the natives and newcomers exchanged ideas and customs, gradually moulded a new society.

The Celts were not organised or unified. The spirit that had led them to dominate much of western Europe was not easily subdued. They defended their settlements against their neighbours and engaged in such pastimes as raiding and cattlerustling as well as friendly trading. Like their counterparts on the Continent, they heralded their many battles with flamboyant displays. A ceremonial trumpet from Deskford (Banff) must have been used to strike fear into the enemies' hearts in the second century AD.

The Celts arrived in Scotland at many different times during the Iron Age; in many cases they were probably fleeing from aggressive neighbours. This was almost certainly true of the owners of a finely decorated torc (neckring) that came to light on a remote hillside at Netherurd (Peeblesshire). This superb piece of craftsmanship is similar to pieces found at Snettisham (Norfolk). At about the time they were made, southern Britain was unsuccessfully fending off Belgic invaders from the Continent. The Netherurd torc could well have been the property of a refugee in the first century BC, driven northwards by the unrest.

About a hundred years later further refugees moved into Scotland, apparently as a result of the expansionist policy of the southern British tribe of the Catuvellauni. A miscellany of objects in Scotland attests the presence of men and women who fled from Tasciovanus, the tribal leader—brooches, a tankard handle and a remarkable series of cauldrons that were thrown into sacred lochs at Carlingwark (Kirkcudbright) and Cockburnspath (Berwickshire) as offerings to the watergods.

The ascendancy of the Celts in Britain could not withstand the organised military strength of the Romans. Although many areas of Scotland in particular lay outside the reach of the Empire, and con-

Plate 1 (above) Bronze-Age stone circle, Callanish (Lewis); *(below)* Temple Wood stone circle (Argyll). The remains of a Bronze-Age burial cairn. The burial cist is in the foreground

Plate 2 *(above)* The Stichill Collar (Roxburghshire). Bronze, second century AD; *(below)* the Broch of Mousa (Shetland)

tinued their traditional way of life, the southern tribes were forced, like those in England, to adapt to Roman overlordship or be suppressed. From the campaigns of the first century AD, the Celtic way of life in the south was interrupted, but in the north traditions continued even into the Middle Ages. Many remains thus had an astonishingly long life, stretching over many periods, with their peak in the Iron Age.

VISIBLE REMAINS

The Scottish countryside abounds in remains of the Iron-Age Celts. Hillforts built of earth or stone, stone huts of different types, the platforms where timber houses once stood, stone broch towers, underground passages and other slighter remains can be seen in almost every county, spanning a period of nearly a thousand years. Strangely, in contrast to preceding periods when the graves are almost the only visible sites, very few Iron-Age burial places are known in Scotland, and fewer still have left any visible trace.

Palisaded Settlements

The earliest Celts in southern Scotland built one or two huts enclosed by a palisade. Dates obtained by the radiocarbon method suggest their first occupation was in the sixth or seventh centuries BC. Craigmarloch Wood (Renfrewshire) has been dated to around 665 BC, for instance. Platform settlements were double-walled timber roundhouses set on 'platforms' cut into hillsides, built at the same time, and can often be seen in the southern lowlands.

Hillforts

Hillforts were also built in the lowlands. At Hownam (Roxburghshire), excavations in 1948 showed that a palisaded settlement on this windswept hill was replaced, perhaps in the fifth century BC, by a fort with a massive, single, stone rampart. Subsequently this was improved with multiple banks and ditches and an elaborate gateway. Thus enlarged, the fort at Hownam continued in use until the coming of the Romans, when the defences were allowed to decay, and over the hilltop

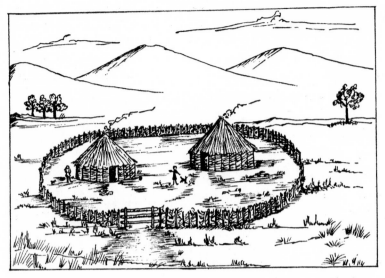

Fig 4   Reconstruction of Glenachan Rig palisaded settlement, Peeblesshire

there spread an open settlement that may have continued into the Dark Ages.

Around 700 BC timber-laced forts had been introduced in north-east Scotland from north Germany. The substantial stone ramparts of these forts were stabilised by a framework of vertical and horizontal beams. In a number of cases the timbers were fired (either accidentally or deliberately by the enemy in a siege), and as the wood burned it created draught channels in the rampart which acted as bellows and heated the stone to a temperature of between 700° and 1,200° C. Where the stone contained a high proportion of silica (for example granite or sandstone) this melted, and the stonework of the rampart fused into a solid mass. Such *vitrified forts* are particularly common in Inverness and Aberdeenshire. Once established, the custom of building timber-laced forts was longlived, and some of the vitrified forts found in Scotland were constructed as late as the Middle Ages. Among the vitrified forts to be explored using modern techniques is Cullykhan (Banff), which seems to have been built in the fifth or sixth century BC with an elaborate timber and stone entrance with a gateway tower. Within this defence were rectangular timber-framed houses.

Crannogs

Not all areas of Scotland have hills suitable for defence. Nor indeed is height necessarily to be equated with safety, and some people, especially in the south, protected themselves by building their houses on artificial platforms or islands in lochs. These crannogs were first popular at the same time as the hillforts, but some may be updated and improved Bronze-Age constructions. The name comes from the old Irish word for a tree (*crann*) and crannogs are particularly common in Ireland. The majority of the excavated Scottish examples belong to the period of Roman military occupation. Only one, at Milton Loch (Kirkcudbright), has been fully excavated recently.

The crannog at Milton Loch was constructed by anchoring a raft of large logs laid radially and concentrically on the marshy loch surface. On this a circular house was built with a surrounding platform joined to the mainland by a causeway. The walls of the house were horizontally laid timbers kept in position by uprights and the roof was thatched. The house was divided by wattle or hurdle partitions, and seems to have had an inner, rectilinear room. It was probably occupied in the second century AD by Celts who had a taste for Roman gew-gaws and lived off the birds that frequented the loch (including cormorants), but who must also have tilled nearby fields, as the finds included part of a plough and a quern for grinding grain.

Dumbuck Crannog, one of a group centred on the Clyde, gained notoriety when many incredible objects were reported to have been found there late last century. These were the outcome of a hoax—every twenty-four hours the site was covered with fresh silt, in which the fakes were hidden. Confusion arose because many of the finds were genuine antiquities, including a ladder and a 32ft long canoe. The unmasking of the Dumbuck forgery stimulated the well-known antiquary Robert Munro to write his book on *Fake Antiquities*.

Thus through the last few centuries BC, defended settlements began to dominate the southern Scottish landscape, acting as tribal centres and

Fig 5 Reconstruction of Milton Loch crannog, Kirkcudbright, in the early second century AD

foci for the subsidiary pattern of farmsteads, which had adapted their form to suit their environment. Nothing is known of the history of this period, but the names of the tribes that had emerged by the first century AD were supplied by the Roman geographer, Ptolemy, who outlined a tribal map which can be filled in from other Classical sources.

Brochs

In the bleak and rocky Western Isles and in Shetland different kinds of forts were built. The first Celtic settlers in the Western Isles had come not by land but by the perilous sea journey along the Atlantic coast of Britain. Some of the pottery from sites such as Dun Mor Vaul (Tiree) hints at contacts even as far afield as western France.

The Hebrideans developed techniques of stone-fort building in response to their rocky environment. They used distinctive hollow walls—double walls with transverse bonding stones. The technique was first developed in the first century BC on Skye, in a series of small forts called *semibrochs*.

Semibrochs developed into *broch towers* around 75 BC, probably in the Hebrides, and thereafter became popular on the northern mainland and the Northern Isles. In Orkney and Shetland the most extreme variants of the broch tradition can be found. In the north mainland and Northern Isles the building of a solid base for the walls was developed in response to the less rugged terrain. The time was ripe for the building of the Broch of Mousa.

Basically, all brochs display similar features. At ground level a dry-stone wall encloses a central court some 25–35ft (7·6–10·6m) in diameter. This wall, about 12ft (3·6m) thick, is usually pierced by a passage with checks and a bar hole for a thick wooden door. Two intra-mural chambers open from the entrance passage. One was originally a guardchamber, the other gave access to an internal staircase. From the first-floor level an inner and an outer casement wall rise up, bonded with transverse slabs, and an internal staircase, to the wall-head. The inner wall-face has a scarcement ledge at a height of about 6ft (1·8m) from the floor, which supported a timber range. Brochs usually had a central well, and eventually had fixed stone furnishings such as water tanks in the floor, slab partition walls, stone cists and fireplaces.

Unlike many archaeological remains, the spread of brochs does not seem to represent the distribution of people. Brochs were built in response to needs dictated by a state of constant feud and warfare between various factions. It is not unreasonable to compare brochs with the castles of the Middle Ages.

Wheelhouses

In about the second century AD brochs were replaced by stone huts of various types. Times were changing, and the threat to the northern warlords seems to have come more from Rome than from neighbouring chiefs. Stone huts were built in the shadow of the brochs, sometimes from the very same stones. Clusters of huts grew up, careless of the danger of falling masonry from the old towers. In some cases these huts lasted until the coming of the Vikings in the eighth century AD.

One of the many types of stone hut is the wheelhouse, a structure with radial piers to support the roof which in plan looks very much like

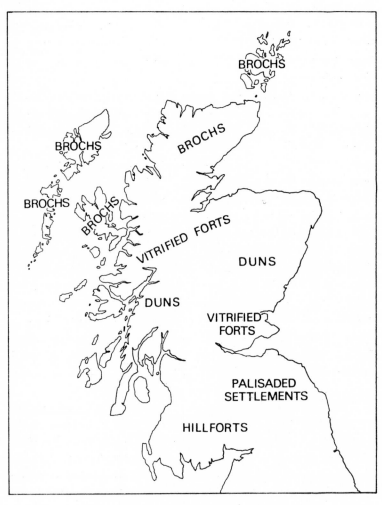

Fig 6 Map of types of Iron-Age monuments

a wheel, the piers being the spokes and the central hearth the hub. These developed in Shetland (where superb examples can be seen at Jarlshof), and subsequently spread to the Hebrides.

Duns

Small stone-walled forts called duns are found in northern Scotland. The most distinctive are *galleried duns*, which have massive walls often as much as 16ft (4·8m) thick, enclosing a courtyard 50ft (15·2m) or more in diameter. They are furnished with a single entrance, checked for a door. Like brochs, they often have galleries or passages inside the walls, and staircases, either inside the wall or in the courtyard, lead to the top. They were never as high as brochs, however, and contained insubstantial huts or shelters. *Promontory duns* are found on rocky headlands, where a thick, galleried wall separated the fort from the mainland. Those built on rock stacks are known as *stack forts*.

Duns are particularly common in the Western Isles and in Argyll, but good examples can also be found in Galloway and Perthshire. Most of them seem to have been occupied around the first century AD.

Souterrains

Souterrains or earth-houses are especially concentrated in Fife and Angus, but there are other distinct groups in Orkney, the north mainland, and south of the Forth–Clyde line. Many rival theories have been put forward about the origin and purpose of these mysterious structures, which usually consist of an underground passage lined with stonework, sometimes terminating in a chamber. Two were excavated in Angus, at Ardestie and Carlungie, and found to have belonged to above-ground huts, long since vanished, occupied in the early centuries AD. Some, such as one at Jarlshof, seem to date to the late Bronze Age, some are possibly as late as the Dark Ages, while others seem to have been re-used in the Middle Ages. Some may have been hiding places in time of trouble, or byres for animals, or possibly cool stores for dairy produce.

Art

Of all the remains of the Iron-Age Celts in Scotland, the most

41

remarkable are objects decorated with their distinctive art. Celtic art represents the greatest contribution of prehistoric Europe to human achievement. It is at once barbaric yet restrained, vigorous yet graceful, flamboyant yet delicate. Like all barbarian art forms it is abstract rather than naturalistic, using for its basic repertoire of motifs spirals, scrolls, voids, pelta patterns and triskeles. The Celts took their inspiration from widely varied sources—Greek art provided human faces, acanthus, vine, palmette and other plant ornament, while Steppe nomads and the East provided animals both natural and exotic, the shapes of which were a springboard from which the Celtic artist could let his imagination dive into a sea of restless, seething line. Celtic art developed on the Continent in the fifth to fourth centuries BC; it came to Britain on imported objects and in the minds of immigrants, and from the third century BC onwards was to take on new forms peculiar to these islands. Insular schools grew up and gave rise to other schools, and this native tradition blossomed in the late first century BC and early first century AD when Caesar's conquest of Gaul had all but stamped it out on the Continent.

Fig 7 Terminal of gold torc or neckring, from Netherurd, Peeblesshire, first century BC

Many imports found their way to south-west Scotland, amongst which excel a delightful little pony cap and pair of drinking-horn mounts from Torrs (Kirkcudbright), that date from around 200 BC. The drinking-horn mounts, with their graceful patterns inlaid with basketry designs, are superb examples of the Celtic bronzesmith's craft. So, too, are a series of first century AD imports from Balmacellan (Kirkcud-bright), which include a mirror decorated in a style popular in south-east England. A bone comb from a crannog at Langbank on the Clyde shows how this art was not confined to rich metalwork, but pervaded everyday life, while a series of distinctive bronze armrings and bracelets from north-east Scotland show that the tradition survived in Scotland into the second century AD. It was a tradition that proved persistent, and reached its greatest maturity in the Christian Dark Ages.

4

THE ROMAN CENTURIES

It is to the marriage of the Roman historian, Tacitus, that we owe the documentation of the Roman conquest of Scotland. His father-in-law was Agricola, the general who led the army through hostile Celtic tribes as far north as Auchinhove (Banff). An account of his life by his son-in-law naturally included the Caledonian campaigns.

The Roman occupation of Britain lasted for nearly four centuries, but so successful were the tribes in Scotland at resisting the might of Rome, that the effective occupation north of the Solway ended towards the end of the second century AD. No town or villa was built in the area and at every opportunity the tribes rose up, sacked forts and raided civilised areas with all the old Celtic spirit of their forefathers.

In AD 43 the Roman forces of the emperor Claudius landed in Kent and within a quarter of a century much of England was subdued, and Rome was ready to annex Scotland. In AD 71 Petillius Cerialis, governor of Britain, possibly campaigned against the Brigantes in the north from the military base at York. Agricola was one of Cerialis' legionary commanders, and, between AD 78 and 84, was governor of Britain. During this time he campaigned vigorously, both in Wales and in Scotland—in AD 79 he left his base at Chester and advanced north through Lancashire to Carlisle. A line of forts was established along the line of the road that is now known as the Stanegate. Scotland was attacked in a pincer movement, Agricola advancing from Carlisle with his second-in-command moving rapidly up the east coast to Newstead until the two forces met up somewhere between the Forth and Clyde. Here Agricola established a series of forts which were later incorporated into what

44

became the Antonine Wall, arguably the greatest Roman achievement in Britain.

From aerial photographs an astonishing picture of the Roman advance can be built up. The network of temporary camps demonstrates Agricola's route around the highlands. Today only the difference in cropmarks shows up the banks and ditches that represent the determination of the Roman general in hostile countryside.

Agricola probably intended to annex all the Scottish mainland, and his success seemed certain in AD 84, after he had put to flight over 30,000 Caledonians at a now unidentified place called Mons Graupius. But it was not to be. Troubles on the Danube frontier led to the withdrawal of one legion and some auxiliaries, Agricola himself being recalled to Rome immediately after the victory. 'Caledonia' was never to be a part of Romanised 'Britannia'.

Scotland was occupied by diminished forces until the reign of the emperor Trajan (AD 98–117), when there were further withdrawals to the Danube frontier. Around this time there were uprisings in northern Britain, and a series of forts, among them Castledykes (Lanarkshire) and Dalswinton and Glenlochar (Dumfriesshire), were burnt down. Why were the forts burnt? This remains one of the great puzzles of Roman archaeology in Scotland. They could have been fired by the native tribes or by the Romans abandoning them to prevent looting or unofficial use. It is not impossible that they were fired by accident—we shall probably never know the real answer.

In AD 122 the emperor Hadrian authorised the construction of the frontier defence known as Hadrian's Wall, between the Tyne and Solway. It did little or nothing to pacify native resistance, and between AD 139 and 142 the governor, Lollius Urbicus, carried out an incisive military campaign in southern Scotland, which was coupled with the construction of a second frontier defence, the Antonine Wall. This was in most ways a tactical improvement on that of Hadrian's Wall, and was intended to replace it, though both were held simultaneously at one stage. Unlike its predecessor, it was built with few changes in construction policy—its thirty-seven miles' (59·5km) length stretched between the Forth and Clyde and its design was dictated by the lessons learned in building Hadrian's Wall. Nowadays the Antonine Wall is mainly unimpressive, partly due to its turf construction and partly because it runs through the heart of industrial Scotland and has been destroyed or despoiled by urban spread. Two main routes led to it—through Annandale and the Clyde valley via the fort of Castledykes in the west, and through Newstead to Inveresk in the east.

The first occupation of the Antonine Wall was probably little more than fifteen years—its forts were burnt, either by the natives or the departing troops. It was reoccupied around AD 158, probably until 163. It is possible that the Romans made a third attempt to fortify it about thirty years later but the evidence is unclear.

An uprising in north-east Scotland of the Caledonii and Maeatae was defeated by a punitive expedition in 209–10 by the emperor Septimius Severus, who died in 211. His son, Caracalla, made peace with the tribes who continued to revolt. From this time on, the area north of Hadrian's Wall was a constant source of trouble to the Romans. There was destruction of this frontier in 296, and outpost forts were destroyed in 342. In 360 disputes involving the Romans and the Scots of Ireland and the Picts of Scotland were settled, but only seven years later these two tribes allied with the Saxons and overran Hadrian's Wall. There were expeditions against these tribes in 395, but by 401 troops were withdrawn from Britain to the Continent and the Roman strength in Britain never recovered. By 410 the emperor Honorius told the British cities to look to their own defence. The Celtic tribes in Scotland continued their development with no further interference from civilisation. Eventually the Scots of Ireland settled in the area around Dunadd (Argyll) and fought constantly, in the true Celtic tradition, with their neighbours, the Picts. South of Hadrian's Wall the Saxons and Angles gradually gained ascendancy.

VISIBLE REMAINS

The Roman occupation of Scotland was military, and accordingly the remains are of forts, camps, roads, signal towers and the frontier work of the Antonine Wall.

The Antonine Wall

The Antonine Wall ran along the slopes of the almost continuous range of hills between the Forth and Clyde. It was built of turf on a stone foundation. Its original height of 10ft (3·05m) with a 6ft (1·8m) high parapet is now badly denuded, and it cannot now be properly appreciated from its remains. To the front ran a ditch some 40ft wide by 12ft deep (12·2 × 3·6m), except where it was hewn less ambitiously from the living rock. Twenty forts housed auxiliary troops from Thrace (on the Black Sea), Gaul, Syria, Spain and the Lower Rhine. The legionary soldiers were of the Second Legion, which was moved north from Caerleon-upon-Usk, and detachments from Chester and York. The small groups of working parties who built the wall left slabs inscribed with their legionary particulars at intervals along the work. Two each of the Twentieth, the Second and the Sixth survive. Thanks to tombstones, the Romans who lived at the frontier and its hinterland sometimes take on identities. Tombstones from a Roman cemetery found in the eighteenth century at Auchendavy commemorate Flavius Lucianus, a private in the Second Legion, a fifteen-year-old boy, Salamanes (perhaps the bastard of a Roman soldier), and a lady, Verecunda.

The Antonine Wall forts vary considerably in size and design—they range from Mumrills (6½ acres) to Duntocher (¼ acre). All had stone principal buildings and wooden barracks, and all had either turf or clay ramparts, with the exception of Castlecary and Balmuildy, which were of stone. Double or triple ditches were normal, and many had fortified annexes, either for military purposes, or possibly to protect the civilian population connected with the forts. On occasion, however, to judge by the finds of children's shoes at Bar Hill, civilians must have lived inside the forts proper.

On the west the Antonine Wall was protected by outpost forts and a signal station, while on the east there were flanking forts at Cramond and Inveresk. A road running northwards into Perthshire cut off Fife from hostile action, and prevented Strathmore from becoming a springboard for revolt.

New discoveries are constantly coming to light along the Antonine Wall. In 1969 a distance slab was found at Hutcheson Hill (Dunbarton), which reports that a detachment of the Second Legion completed 3,000ft (915m) of the wall, and bears a puzzling scene which has been interpreted as a personification of the province of Britain congratulating the Roman army on having added the area between the two walls to the empire and (hopefully, if inaccurately) thus making it civilised. The same year brought to light an altar at Old Kilpatrick, dedicated by the first cohort of the Baetasians to Jupiter, explaining further that the cohort was under the command of Publicius Maternus and the prefect who was responsible to the centurion of the First Italic Legion. The First Legion was based in Moesia (modern Bulgaria) and the circumstances in which a detachment from this legion could be present in Britain are difficult to guess. One expert has suggested that it could only have happened in 208–10, when the emperor Septimius Severus was campaigning in Britain, but if this is so, it would suggest the Antonine Wall was still being garrisoned then, which is a direct contradiction of the generally held view that the wall was abandoned by about 187. It is through such apparently tiny clues that the history of Roman Britain is constantly being rewritten.

In 1973 a fort was discovered in the Glasgow suburb of Bearsden. Traces of it had been recorded in 1755 and 1862, but it was believed to have been destroyed by Victorian villas and gardens. As it happened, part of the site had been built up into clay terraces, and thus was cocooned and protected for posterity. The finest Roman bath-house to be discovered in Scotland survived in places up to eight courses high at Bearsden, and still retained some of its original wall and floor plaster. Among the finds was a stone fountainhead which reminds us that even in the most north-westerly corner of the Roman Empire the standards of civilisation were maintained.

Forts, Camps and Roads

Forts were the permanent or semi-permanent bases of the army, and are usually rectangular with curved corners. On the ground they are normally recognisable by the banks and ditches of the defences—they

48

may have a single ditch or (exceptionally) up to seven—and as a rule have a pair of opposed entrances in both long and short sides. In Scotland they range widely in size, from the enormous 53-acre Inchtuthil (Perthshire) which housed about 6,000 legionaries, to small fortlets like the recently excavated and now destroyed example at Barburgh Mill (Dumfriesshire, ⅓ acre) which could have housed only one infantry unit.

The earliest forts had turf defences and timber buildings, but by the second century the principal buildings in many forts were of stone and sometimes stone facings were added to the rampart. In a few forts, such as Birrens (Dumfriesshire), all the buildings were of stone. Most had bath-houses outside the defences, because of the risk of fire. Except from those on the Antonine Wall and at Cramond there are almost no traces above ground of internal fort buildings. One of the best preserved fort defensive works can be seen at Ardoch (Perthshire).

Camps were temporary constructions, thrown up at the end of a day's march to be abandoned next day, and their distribution thus demonstrates much about the army's movements. Each soldier carried a trenching tool and a couple of stakes and dug a section of ditch, throwing the spoil up to form a bank on which he set his stakes. Thus a continuous earthwork was crowned by a palisade of stakes to protect the leather tents. Such temporary camps, though bounded by straight lines, are often of irregular shape, usually because of the terrain.

Signal stations were used for sending messages. The most famous series runs along the Roman road which follows the Gask ridge (Perthshire)—there are ten along eight miles of road. They consisted of a wooden tower about 10ft (3·04m) square surrounded by a circular ditch about 12ft (3·6m) across, enclosing an area 30–40ft (9·1–12·2m) in diameter, though they can vary greatly (the Gask stations are fairly uniformly 100ft (30·5m) across overall).

Roads connected the main forts, and can often be traced for considerable distances. A good section of the road into Scotland known as Dere Street can be seen adjacent to the Iron-Age fort of Woden Law.

Everyday Life

There are very good collections of Roman objects in the National Museum of Antiquities of Scotland in Edinburgh and the Hunterian Museum at Glasgow University, while a few other Roman finds can be seen in Dumfries Burgh Museum and in Dundee Museum.

The fort of Newstead (Roxburghshire) has produced more Roman finds than any other in the north-west of the Roman Empire, and these can be seen in Edinburgh. Particularly interesting are the fragments of leather—tents, boots and shoes, and a horse chamfrein. Of the pieces of Roman armour from the site, the most impressive are the parade helmets with human faces as vizors. Bronze jugs and camp kettles, brooches, glassware and a wide array of tools are on display, as well as the inevitable pottery and coins. There are also wooden writing tablets and the bronze *styli* used for writing on the wax with which they were once coated.

The most spectacular Roman find from Scotland is the Traprain treasure. This vast hoard of silverwork of the late fourth century, found in the Iron-Age hillfort of Traprain Law, can be seen in the National Museum. It weighs over 770 oz troy, and consists of over 100 different objects, mostly very fragmentary, including dishes, plates, bowls, flagons, cups and spoons. It is badly crushed, and seems to have been deliberately broken and bent, ready for the melting pot—presumably it had been taken as loot from a rich household in England or Gaul.

The Hunterian Museum has a good collection of finds from the Antonine Wall, including sculptures and inscriptions. Among the finds from the fort at Bar Hill can be seen the wheel of a chariot and the remains of a barrel on which the owner had scratched his name—'Ianuarius'.

Plate 3 (above) Interior of a wheelhouse (Jarlshof, Shetland); *(below)* the Antonine Wall and ditch (Falkirk, Stirlingshire)

Plate 4 (above) Bath house of Antonine-Wall fort after excavation (Bearsden, Glasgow); *(below)* citadel of the Scottish kings of Dalriada (Dunadd, Argyll)

5

PICTS AND BRITONS

In summer the picturesque coastal village of Rockcliffe, in the Stewartry of Kirkcudbright, is crowded with holidaymakers. Within walking distance, at low tide, is the National Trust bird sanctuary of Heston Isle, and over the horizon can be seen the hills of Cumbria and the Galloway coast, stretching away amid trees into the blue-grey distance. Inland is Dalbeattie forest from which rises the neo-Gothic form of the Baron's Craig. Between forest and coast, and commanding views of both, is the Mote of Mark, an acre of exposed rock which was the scene of a violent conflict in the centuries immediately following the departure of the Romans.

What happened in Scotland after the legions finally marched south? From many points of view the land and people had been little changed by the military occupation—men continued to herd their cattle and tend their fields. But Rome had made some irreversible changes. Many Roman everyday objects had been gradually adapted by the northern tribesmen—technology had improved (especially metalworking) and weapons were modelled on those of Roman legionaries. On a subtler level the ideas of Roman provincial administration had taken root. In the troublesome years of the late fourth century, when the Roman Empire was under threat of invasion from all sides, the relatively friendly frontier chiefs had been encouraged to defend their territories in the name of Rome against enemies often only slightly more barbarian than they were themselves.

Even after the legions had withdrawn to the Continent, Celtic chiefs in Scotland still modelled themselves on the Romans and continued the defence of their 'Roman' kingdoms against incoming oppressors. Such

D

a leader in England was the legendary Arthur, who tried to hold back the advancing Anglo-Saxons in the late fifth century. A century later, Urien, King of Rheged, similarly attempted to withstand the Angles in south-west Scotland.

By the fifth century the Celts of Scotland were arranged into two predominant groups. To the north of the Forth–Clyde line were the Picts: to the south of them were the Britons. The Britons formed themselves into kingdoms, the origins of which were rooted in the late days of Roman Britain, and whose rulers traced their lines back to men with Roman names. Nevertheless, the territories of these kingdoms approximated to the old tribal areas that had faced the Romans. The native Picts and Britons had to defend their territories against the Scots from Ireland and the Angles who had settled in the old Roman areas. The Scots formed a kingdom of Dalriada, based on Dunadd (Argyll), and menaced the Picts in particular. The Angles attacked the Britons especially. Finally the Vikings arrived from Scandinavia, first to raid and then to settle. In the early ninth century the Vikings terrorised Picts, Scots and Angles alike.

The Mote of Mark lay in the heart of the British kingdom of Rheged, which extended from south of Carlisle in a broad sweep to Galloway. In the fifth century the Britons built a timber-laced rampart around the top of the rock to protect their workshops and homes. By the late sixth century Rheged was very powerful under the leadership of its most famous king, Urien, and the Mote of Mark probably reflected the prosperity of the whole kingdom as the scene of tremendous industry. Gold, silver, bronze, brass, lead and iron were worked, often into objects of exquisite beauty. Then the blow fell. Urien, who had held back the advancing tide of Angles for many years, was killed through treachery, and the frontiers were breached. At the Mote of Mark, in spite of a hurried attempt to block the gateway with an emergency rampart, the fort was destroyed. The stonework of the rampart melted in the conflagration into pumice-like lumps and the defences were subsequently dismantled. The vitrified stone was rolled over the side of the rock where it remains to this day.

A few finds suggest the Angles held the site for a while at least—they

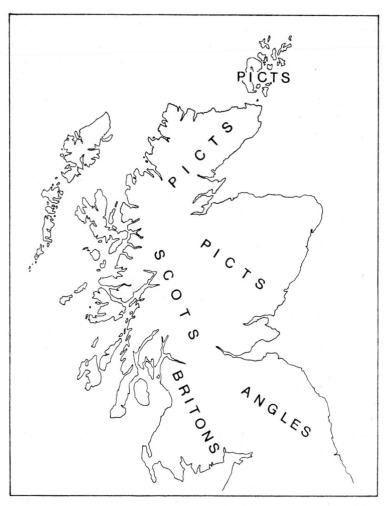

Fig 8   Map of Dark-Age Scotland

include inscriptions in Anglian runes, one of which is part of a personal name—'Athili'.

The Welsh poet, Llywarch Hen, who had been in Urien's court, describes the ruin of his master's stronghold. Although it is unlikely that the Mote of Mark was the king's own seat the description is uncannily similar to the picture that emerged during the 1973 excavations. The poet mourns the heap of rubble that was once Urien's court, and the hearth, once ablaze with logs heating the cauldrons, now green with weed and covered with bugloss and dock leaves. The entire site, narrates the poet, which was once bright and gay with the shouts of warriors, has become a floor where pigs rootle and birds peck.

THE BRITONS

Visible Remains

There are very few clear remains of the Britons in southern Scotland. Apart from the Mote of Mark, there are a number of hillfort capitals, but few of these have any visible mark of the period because of disturbance by medieval and later structures. The capital of the kingdom of Strathclyde at Dumbarton Rock, for instance, is now mostly covered by Dumbarton Castle, while Edinburgh Castle probably shrouds the site of a Dark-Age settlement. Some Iron-Age hillforts have additions which may belong to the Dark Ages, such as the latest rampart at Traprain Law (East Lothian), or parts of Chatto Craig or Penniel Heugh (Roxburghshire).

A few small forts such as Trusty's Hill (Anwoth, Kirkcudbrightshire) may have been occupied in the Dark Ages—Pictish symbols, possibly the work of a raiding party, were carved into a rock on the hill.

The Britons continued to occupy crannogs or lake dwellings, but made no outstanding changes to them. An important crannog, occupied in the seventh century, was excavated at Buston (Ayrshire) in the nineteenth century, but, in common with most such sites, little is visible now.

Everyday Life

Most of our knowledge of the everyday life of the Britons comes from finds from the Mote of Mark and Buston crannog, many of which are on display in the National Museum in Edinburgh. The most interesting finds from the Mote of Mark are clay moulds for casting brooches, pins and a host of other objects, many of them richly decorated with interlace patterns. Ironwork from the two sites included part of a padlock of Roman type, tweezers, part of a horse's bit, chisels, a spearhead and arrows, an axe, knives and various mounts. Two gold spiral rings were found at Buston, as well as bone combs. Both sites yielded pottery imported from France, and the Mote of Mark produced fragments of glass from the Rhineland, indicative of trade with these areas. The array of finds suggests that the upper strata of society at least, enjoyed a standard of living substantially higher than one might first expect from the small traces of structures of the period.

THE PICTS

The Picts are one of the most romantic-sounding peoples of British antiquity, ranking on a par with the Druids and King Arthur. Popularly and traditionally they were small, dark men who covered themselves with tattoos and constantly raided Hadrian's Wall and the north of England from their forest fastnesses in Dark-Age Scotland. As might be imagined, this is only half the truth, for whilst the Picts undoubtedly led expeditions against the Romans, they were certainly no less advanced than any of their contemporaries, and were flourishing long after the wind had started to blow leaves and earth over the crumbling and abandoned forts of Hadrian's Wall.

It is in the pages of Roman literature that the Picts make their initial historical appearance. They were first positively mentioned around the end of the third century AD, and thereafter appear regularly amongst the barbarian raiders of Roman Britain.

No document (except a list of Pictish kings) has survived in Pictish, and our understanding of their language is confined to what linguists can infer from a few personal names and place-names, along with two or three words that have survived in inscriptions. It is this lack of contemporary Pictish documentation that has moulded the Picts into an enigmatic and mysterious race.

The evidence of archaeology suggests that the Picts were the descendants of the Caledonians and Maeatae. The conquest of the Picts by their ancient enemies, the Scots of the west Highlands, resulted in a unified Scotland under Kenneth mac Alpin in the ninth century.

Visible Remains

If the Picts have left no memorials to their existence in the pages of history, they have left traces in their hillforts, their metalwork and, possibly most significantly of all, in the indecipherable symbols carved in stone that are scattered over the Scottish countryside north of the Forth.

Forts

The Picts occupied craggy fortified rocks and sometimes re-used earlier Iron-Age forts. A characteristic feature of Pictish defence was the construction of short stretches of rampart to link natural defences such as steep, rock outcrops, known as *nuclear forts*. A series of 'courts' with staggered entrances led ultimately to a citadel on the highest point of the hill. Examples can be seen at Moncrieffe Hill and Dundurn (Perthshire) and at Dumyat (Stirlingshire). Traditional timber-laced forts were still built in Pictland in the post-Roman period. The fort at Burghead (Moray), for instance, was provided with such ramparts by the Picts.

Pictish houses have not survived well—the remains of one within a timber-laced fort was excavated at Cullykhan (Banff). It was rectangular, of timber, and had a porch. At Clatchard's Craig (Fife), a fort was reoccupied by the Picts who built a timber hall there and constructed a new rampart using old Roman masonry.

Everyday Things

The Picts imported pottery from the region around Bordeaux, and used composite bone combs, glass beads and spindle whorls. In the fifth and sixth centuries, too, much of their metalwork was similar to that used by the Scots or the Britons. The Picts inherited a love of naturalistic representations of animals from their Caledonian ancestors, and rapidly took to copying animal forms from imported late-Roman or continental metalwork. They favoured buckles and swivel rings with confronted animal heads and, later, lively yapping animals. These they engraved lightly on a variety of objects, from the Monymusk Reliquary (see p 67), to a bucket found in a Scandinavian grave that had obviously been looted by Vikings. The Picts, too, made hanging bowls—bronze with openwork or enamelled escutcheons on the base and rims to take chains for suspension. A mould for a hanging-bowl escutcheon has been found at Craig Phadrig (Inverness), while fragments of the bowls them-selves have turned up as part of hoards at Tummel Bridge (Perthshire) and Castle Tioram (Inverness).

Pictish skill in metalworking reached its peak in the eighth century with the production of a magnificent series of silver brooches and a companion series in bronze. The brooches are based on the penannular types current from the Iron Age in Britain, but the Picts gave them distinctive treatment. One of the finest comes from Rogart (Suther-land), and is decorated with birds' heads in relief, pecking at ornamental roundels. The most famous series comes from the St Ninian's Isle treasure, found in 1958 during excavations at an early church site on this tiny tidal island off the coast of Shetland. Buried around AD 800, in the face of a Viking raid, the hoard consisted of a rich variety of superb silver objects—beaten silver bowls, a spoon with a dog's head licking from the bowl, a pronged implement, a pair of sword chapes (one with a Pictish inscription), a sword pommel and a silver hanging bowl. All, with the possible exception of the hanging bowl, which may have been made in Northumbria, were the products of Pictish craftsmen. Along with the Anglo-Saxon treasure of Sutton Hoo, the St Ninian's Isle treasure ranks as one of the greatest art treasures to come from British soil.

Naturalistic animals are seen even more confidently displayed on the mysterious symbol stones erected in Pictland. The earliest are simply rough stones incised with animal and abstract symbols. Dressed stones with relief sculpture were produced slightly later and consist chiefly of cross-slabs (a Christian cross forming the main element of the design) which display mysterious symbols in relief. Latterly, after the eclipse of the historical kingdom of the Picts, some craftsmen still kept alive the old traditions, and put up stones with accomplished relief carving, but lacking the symbols.

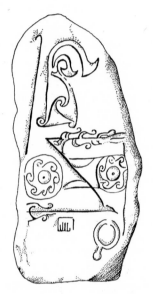

Fig 9   Pictish symbol stone, Dunnichen, Angus

What kind of symbols are they? First there is a series of animals, nearly eleven of which would have roamed the Pictish forests—boars, deer, wolves—or would have been found in the rivers, such as the salmon. Only two beasts are mythical, the 'swimming elephant' as it is called and the 'S-dragon'. Apart from these there are abstract symbols, known as 'V-rod and crescent', 'notched rectangle', or 'triple disc' according to their shape. It has been suggested that the Pictish symbol stones are tombstones, and that the symbols are clan badges or badges denoting rank. But they are not usually found over graves, and the

60

Plate 5 (above) The Hunterston Brooch (Ayrshire), *c* AD 800. Silver; *(below)* the Mote of Mark. Citadel, fifth–sixth century AD

Plate 6 (above) The Pictish
Aberlemno Churchyard Cross.
Eighth century; *(right)* the Anglian
Ruthwell Cross (detail). Seventh
century

Plate 7 *(above)* Caerlaverock Castle (Dumfriesshire); *(below)* the Kames Brooch. *c* AD 1300. Gold

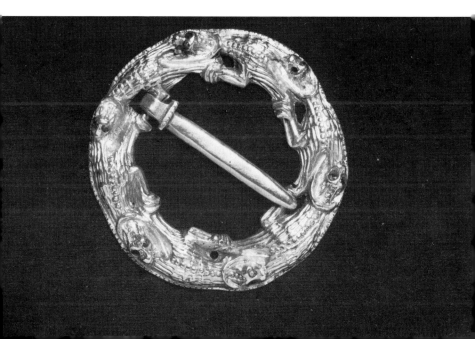

Plate 8 (above) Lochmaben Castle (Dumfriesshire). Fourteenth century; *(below)* Threave Castle (Kirkcudbright). Fourteenth century

symbols themselves appear on a variety of objects, including the terminal rings of massive silver chains, on silver ornamental plates, on bones, and even on pin heads. They could have been marks of ownership, and the stones could have been set up to mark territorial boundaries, but we can do no more than speculate.

CHRISTIANITY

Iona, so medieval legend has it, was the first place to be created and will be the last place to be destroyed. Lying some thirty-five miles off the coast of the Scottish mainland, east of Tiree, it is a small island difficult of access in all but the calmest weather. As boats approach across the waters, the first sight of human activity on the island is the Benedictine priory, founded in the late twelfth century, the conventual buildings of which have been largely rebuilt by the modern Iona Community. It is a tranquil place, that betrays nothing of its varied history. Here the gentle Irish monk, Columba, came to found his monastery in about AD 563, and here, in the ninth century, the Vikings wreaked havoc.

Most of the remains of Iona belong to the medieval and later periods, but it is still possible to trace the bank or *vallum* of the original monastery and to marvel at the fine, free-standing, high crosses of St Martin and St John (the latter recently superbly restored) set up in the ninth century by the monks. Visitors can see a cell where, traditionally, St Columba lived, though its genuine association with the saint is far from certain.

Christianity probably came to North Britain with the Roman army, and was kept alive at the western end of Hadrian's Wall by civilians living around Carlisle. It is probable that, before the end of the fourth century, a further outpost of Christian belief had been established in the neighbourhood of Whithorn (Wigtownshire), and possibly even further north. This existing tradition of Christianity no doubt provided the seed which grew and spread in the fifth and sixth centuries, and it is not surprising to find that initially the early Church in Scotland followed the Roman model of a diocesan structure. The dioceses were replaced by a system in which major monasteries were responsible for smaller monasteries, hermitages and church or chapel sites. The Pictish Church, and the Church of the Scots of Dalriada were probably monastic from the outset.

VISIBLE REMAINS

The visible remains of early Christianity in Scotland fall into two categories; the sites of monasteries and churches, which are seldom more than low foundations and banks in the turf, and sculptured stones, some of which still stand where they were erected, but many of which are now in museum collections.

Ecclesiastical Buildings

Monasticism was a Mediterranean idea, and Celtic monasteries were eremetic. Various buildings were scattered about a large enclosure demarcated by a bank or wall (*vallum*). As in the Mediterranean, the first Celtic monasteries, such as Iona, had rectilinear enclosures. Later both monasteries and churchyards were delimited by a circular bank, examples of which are visible at Applecross (Wester Ross) and (under the later churchyard wall) at Papil in Shetland.

The earliest ecclesiastical buildings were of timber and have not survived (they are known to have existed from excavations at Ardwall Island, Kirkcudbright); only a few stone-built, eighth-century and later structures remain. At the small monastery at Eileach an Naomh in the Garvellochs, stone-built monks' cells with corbelled roofs of beehive shape remain, similar to some in Ireland. The stone foundations of a small rectangular chapel are above ground at Chapel Finian (Mochrum, Galloway) which was probably set up by Irish settlers. Even if the remains are slight, its setting on a main road looking out across a scenic bay make it worth a visit.

Attached to Brechin Cathedral (Angus) is a round tower with a carved entrance set above ground level. Originally free-standing, the tower dates from about AD 1000. Abernethy Round Tower is the only other

66

survivor of this period in Scotland, and stands in the churchyard, not far from a Pictish symbol stone.

A few caves are associated with early saints, of which the most famous is St Ninian's Cave at Physgyll (near Whithorn). A fine collection of sculptured stones of Dark-Age date, from this cave, are displayed in Whithorn Museum.

Objects in Museums

Reliquaries are containers for relics of early saints. Of these the superb Monymusk Reliquary (the Brecbennoch), now in the National Museum in Edinburgh, is outstanding. Probably of seventh-century date, this house-shaped shrine may have held a relic of St Columba. It was carried into battle by the Scots when they defeated the English at Bannockburn in 1314.

The sculptured stones of Scotland are the most impressive remains of early Christianity. The most abundant are the cross-slabs of Pictland (see p 60), large and important collections of which are housed in museums at Meigle (Perthshire) and St Vigeans (Angus), but there are other outstanding examples of stone carving in other areas. The finest are the superb free-standing crosses of Iona (see p 65). Of these, St John's and St Martin's crosses are covered with spirals and other complex patterns which combine with bosses and other ornamentation to produce an integrated and satisfying whole. The early Iona crosses themselves are devoid of scriptural ornament, but figural work can be seen on a related piece, the cross at Kildalton (Islay).

In the early Christian sculpture from Scotland can be seen the supreme contribution of the Christian Celts to civilisation. There is nothing from Dark-Age Europe to compare with the restrained intricacy of ornament displayed on St John's Cross, and indeed few art styles anywhere at any period have mastered abstract design so that the whole is as satisfying as the endless surprises hidden in this detail. It is hardly surprising, therefore, that copies of St Martin's Cross (even blindly imitating its now damaged arms) can be seen in modern cemeteries and used as war memorials all over Britain, and that jewellery inspired by this 'Celtic' art can be bought in virtually any tourist shop in Scotland.

6

SCOTS, ANGLES AND VIKINGS

If any site can be said to symbolise the growth of Scotland it is Dunadd, in the Crinan Moss of Argyll. Even today it has an air of special importance, thrusting its loaf-shaped rock out of the flat, surrounding fields that once were treacherous bog. The climb to the summit, which takes one through a series of outer courtyards by a steep path, is not easy in summer and daunting in winter when made slippery by rain or sleet. The defences make skilful use of the natural rock outcrop, which is linked by stretches of walling, and the overall plan depends on a central citadel on the highest part of the rock.

Why should this lonely outcrop be so significant? The answer lies in the fact that it was the royal citadel of the Scots, who gave Scotland her name and national language, Scots Gaelic.

THE SCOTS

Ironically the Scots were not natives, but settlers from Ireland. Their name, Scotti, means 'bandits', but the word is Irish rather than British in origin and must have been used to describe the Scotti as they left their homeland in Ulster to found a kingdom known as Dalriada, centred on Argyll. It suggests a picture of wild rovers and seadogs, driven from their home to pioneer new lands. If traditions are correct, the first settlers were few in number, and if the land they had chosen for their landfall had not been sparsely populated, the history of Scotland in subsequent centuries might have been very different. As it was, 150 men, under the leadership of Fergus, managed to carve out a foothold, and in the fullness of time Dunadd became the focus for a dynamic, restless kingdom that constantly pressed on the boundaries of its eastern neighbour, Pictland.

VISIBLE REMAINS

Except at Dunadd, almost nothing remains to be seen of the structures of the ancient Scots. They are certainly the most sparsely represented of all the peoples of Scotland in archaeology. In some measure, however, Dunadd makes up for the absence of other remains. Near the summit of the rock, now protected by a glass frame, a Pictish-looking boar, carved on the living rock, forages near a foot-shaped depression cut into the stone. Here, tradition has it, the kings of the Scots stood to be crowned centuries before the Stone of Destiny became a symbol of Scottish kingship. Adjacent to these carvings is an inscription in the ogham alphabet—a script devised in Ireland which represents letters by vertical strokes along a horizontal bar. It might not at first seem surprising to find an inscription in an old Irish alphabet in this Irish colony, especially since the Scots continued to maintain close links with their homeland, but strangely the inscription is in the Pictish type of ogham. Could it have been carved by a triumphant Pictish rading-party, and could the boar, too, have been their work, a declaration of a hard-won victory about which history is silent? We can only surmise.

The only other remains of the early Scots comprise a few duns (p 41), which the Scots sometimes seem to have taken over and occupied. The most famous is Kildonan, excavated at the outbreak of World War II.

Everyday Things

The finds excavated at Dunadd, at the end of the nineteenth century and between the two world wars, tell us something about the everyday life of the first Scots.

The most informative finds are connected with metalworking. Numerous clay moulds were used to cast bronze brooches and pins, and crucibles for melting the bronze were also unearthed. A fascinating discovery was an artist's sketch for a brooch, scratched on a stone preparatory to making a mould. Although the drawing is crude, it is

Fig 10 Reconstruction of the dun at Kildonan, Argyll, in the seventh century AD

recognisable, from brooches that have been discovered elsewhere. This carving, and one other, is Viking in style, and suggests that wild Norsemen from the Hebrides may have captured the rock in the ninth century.

Fragments of pottery hint at links far afield. Some pots were produced in France, and must have been traded across the stormy Irish Sea to grace the tables of the Scottish kings.

Ironwork shows that the Scots were farmers and craftsmen as well as soldiers. Tools include saws and gouges, and the site produced an enormous number of querns for grinding grain, presumably grown in fields some distance away, as the site was surrounded by marsh.

A stone disc with an inscription '*IN NOMINE*' (*Dei*) shows that by the seventh century, if not before, the Scots were Christians, and an enamelled disc and attractive bronze pin with a head rather like a hand show that the finer arts were not forgotten.

THE ANGLES

Ruthwell is just like any other small parish church. It is approached along narrow, winding roads that are flanked by trees and fields. One comes upon it suddenly, a small grey building surrounded by tombstones. There is nothing extraordinary about the church, it is not even particularly old, and there are many finer in this part of Dumfriesshire. What is remarkable is the Ruthwell Cross, possibly the finest piece of monumental sculpture that has come down to us from the Dark Ages.

Once in the churchyard, but now inside the church to protect it from further weathering, the 15ft-high sandstone cross is remarkably fresh in its carving. It has no predecessors. Set up in the seventh century by the Anglo-Saxons, its inspiration comes not from the Anglo-Saxon world or the Celtic, but from the east Mediterranean, the world of Byzantium. However, its themes are not Byzantine, and the individual designs are without parallel. They speak of qualities dear to the Celtic saints and the early hermits; the qualities of the simple, humble life led in solitude, of life dedicated to God. It depicts the desert fathers, SS Paul and Anthony, Christ, having His feet dried by Mary Magdalene with her hair, and with His feet resting on beasts. On the sides are vinescroll ornaments with birds and animals—(inhabited vinescroll) the ornament that was to become so beloved of Northumbrian sculptors. Inscriptions in runic characters and in Latin letters run in panels up the sides. Among them is a text of the Anglo-Saxon poem *The Dream of the Rood*

Then the young hero—he was God Almighty—firm and unflinching stripped Himself; He mounted on the high cross, brave in the sight of many, when He was minded to redeem mankind. Then I trembled when the Hero clasped me; yet I durst not bow to the earth, fall to the level of the ground, but I must needs stand firm.

This remarkable monument was erected by the Angles and shows the extent to which they had become established in the south-west by about AD 700, about a century after their first advances into the area. With the relentless drive that led them to capture Edinburgh in AD 637, they successfully resisted all attempts to expel them from the south-west. From the seventh century onwards, a hostility grew up which was not lessened until the unification of Scotland and England under James I and VI in 1603, and which suffered further aggravation spasmodically until the present day.

VISIBLE REMAINS

There are almost no visible remains of the Angles in Scotland, in spite of the fact that they were an important element in the history of southern Scotland for many centuries. One probable reason for this is that there were relatively few Angles living in Scotland; they were simply overlords.

The only Anglian site that can be visited at present is Doon Hill (Dunbar, East Lothian), where archaeologists excavated the post-holes of two timber halls, one British and one Anglian. The position of the timbers is marked with concrete pegs and there is an explanatory plan on the site.

There are, however, a number of fine, sculptured stones of the Anglian period still to be seen. Many of these are in museums—the best collections are in the National Museum of Antiquities in Edinburgh, in Dumfries Burgh Museum and in the Whithorn Priory museum (Wigtown). A very interesting collection can be seen in Abercorn Church (Midlothian).

Of the stones in museum collections, particularly interesting is the slab from Jedburgh which appears to be part of a stone church-screen—it is technically almost as good as the Ruthwell Cross, and displays inhabited vinescroll. It is now in the Edinburgh collection. Another fine series of stones come from Hoddom (Dumfriesshire) and are now in Dumfries Museum. Many were found built into the wall of Hoddom Church. Most of the stones in Whithorn belong to a late period of Anglian occupation, and many show the influence of Viking art. Typical of the Whithorn stones are flattish crosses with wheel heads and interlacing on the front—one of the best comes from Kirkinner (Wigtownshire).

A few Anglo-Saxon coins and other objects have been found in

Plate 9 (above) Egilsay Church (Orkney). Twelfth century; *(below)* Loch Leven Castle (Kinross). Fourteenth century

Plate 10 The Prentice Pillar (Roslin Chapel, Midlothian). Fifteenth century

Scotland, and most of these are now in the National Museum in Edinburgh. One gold and garnet pyramid for a sword belt of the seventh
century is very similar to those found in the famous royal Saxon ship-
burial at Sutton Hoo (East Anglia). The Scottish find was from Dalmeny
(East Lothian).

THE VIKINGS

Each day, with a roar of engines, planes sweep down over Sumburgh
Head in Shetland to touch down on the main runway for the Shetland
Isles. As they do so they almost brush the walls of one of the most
amazing archaeological sites in the British Isles—Jarlshof. On this site
there is an almost unbroken history of human occupation, from the time
of the first farmers in Shetland to the seventeenth century, with breaks
only for short periods in the Iron and Middle Ages. Even since the
seventeenth century the site has not been totally abandoned, for nearby
is a nineteenth-century hotel and, of course, Sumburgh Airport. Today
the visitor can see, in an area of about three acres, the grass-topped walls
of the successive settlements. He can step into Bronze-Age houses, still
surviving more or less to roof height, and wander into wheelhouses,
imagining himself back in the time when they were occupied and fires
burned on the still-reddened hearths. But it is the remains of Viking
Jarlshof that are the most extensive, and the maze of walls tell a story of
centuries of Norse occupation.

The coming of the Vikings was heralded by attacks on northern
monasteries. Lindisfarne, off the coast of Northumbria, was sacked in
793, and Iona at the beginning of the ninth century. Almost as early as
the first raids were the first settlements. The first target was Orkney,
which was settled around AD 800 by colonists from Norway. From there
the Norse spread out, colonising Shetland and the north Scottish mainland, particularly Caithness, and extensively occupied the Western
Isles. The subsequent settlement of the Isle of Man and Ireland led to
parts of Galloway being raided and settled by fierce Norse-Irish, who
earned a reputation for being even more savage than the original
Vikings themselves.

E

Under Earl Sigurd the Mighty, Orkney became a Norse earldom around 880 owing only nominal allegiance to the kings of Norway or Scotland. This earldom endured until the thirteenth century, taking under its influence the rest of the Northern Isles and Caithness, and occasionally even the Hebrides. The Norse in Scotland became converted to Christianity under Earl Thorfinn in the eleventh century, during which period the superb Romanesque cathedral of St Magnus was erected in Kirkwall.

The Norse seem to have settled in well with the fairly sparse populations in the Hebrides, Caithness and Orkney. Place-names show how extensive the Norse cultural overlay was in the north—99 per cent of Orkney farm names are Scandinavian in origin, and 80 per cent of Lewis place-names are Norse.

VISIBLE REMAINS

The visible remains of the Viking settlements are almost entirely confined to the Northern Isles. A Norse settlement was excavated at Freswick Links (Caithness), but nothing of it remains to be seen above the sand-dunes, and the other known Norse dwellings in the Hebrides are likewise barely recognisable on the ground. In some areas burial mounds are visible which may be those of Vikings, but most have not been excavated and are therefore not definitely of this period.

Houses

The houses of the Vikings can be seen as grassy foundations on several sites in the Northern Isles. The most famous are those at Jarlshof (Shetland) and Birsay (Orkney).

The Norse introduced new building traditions to Scotland. Whereas before, houses had been mostly circular, the Norse introduced the long rectangular dwelling, often divided with a cross-passage into a living-room and a byre for the animals. The Norse houses in the Northern Isles differ from those in Norway, and it may be that Pictish building traditions played a part in their modification. They were often built with stone inner and outer wall-facings with turf cores to act as insulation—an ancient precursor of the cavity-wall insulation of today. At Jarlshof the first house was 70ft (21·3m) long with slightly bowed sides. In this case the animals seem to have been housed in a separate byre, and the second room in the house was a kitchen, with a separate door opening. There were hearths in both living-room and kitchen, and the living-room had benches of stone along each side, on which tables and beds would have been set. Beyond the houses were other buildings, including sauna-bath houses, temples and barns.

Birsay possesses a palace complex known as Earl Sigurd's Hall, and the remains of another drinking-hall was found at Orphir on the Orkney mainland.

Churches

A few Norse churches survive in Orkney. The finest is perhaps at Egilsay, with its Irish-style round tower attached to the main body of the church, while a tiny round church with apsidal chancel at Orphir may have been inspired by the Church of the Holy Sepulchre in Jerusalem.

The most impressive remains of Norse Christianity are to be seen at Birsay. Here, on a tidal island, which is now approached at low tide across a zigzag causeway, are the ruins of a fine eleventh-century cathedral. Adjacent to it is the bishop's palace, now little more than foundations, and the remains of the graveyard. The whole complex was built upon a Pictish site.

Everyday Life

A fine array of objects of the Viking period greets the visitor to the National Museum of Antiquities in Edinburgh, and other Norse-period objects can be seen in the museums in Kirkwall and Lerwick.

It is the treasure hoards of Viking date that most readily fire the imagination, and best symbolise the traditional picture of the Viking Age. Although there are a few finds from the Hebrides and the Scottish mainland, by far the greater number come from Orkney. The finest is the Skaill Hoard, found in 1858 by a boy out rabbiting. It comprised in all nearly 15lb (6·8k) of silver, made up of 9 brooches, 14 necklets,

27 armlets and 18 whole or fragmentary coins, which dated the hoard to the late tenth century.

From a grave at Westness on Rousay (Orkney) has come a superb Celtic brooch, and other Celtic objects were found during excavation of the cemetery at Pierowall (Orkney) in the last century. Orkney provides evidence of women being killed to accompany their men to the afterlife, a custom fairly rare in the Viking world, but also found in the Isle of Man.

Many finds come from Norse-period burials. The richest have been found in the Hebrides, such as the burial of a man and a horse in a boat at Kiloran Bay (Colonsay), which dated from the late ninth century. The skeleton was accompanied by a sword, shield, cauldron, spear, axe, arrowheads, knife, sickle, whetstone, dress pin, strap mountings, buckle and a set of beam scales and weights. Some of these objects were the products of Celtic workshops: Celtic finds are commonplace in Viking burials, no doubt, in many cases, ill-gotten gains from raids.

In contrast, the finds from Jarlshof and other house sites reflect the peaceful side of Norse life—bone combs, soapstone bowls and lamps, dress pins, and even stone gaming boards.

7

MEDIEVAL SCOTLAND– THE KINGS AND THE CLANS

Lochmaben Castle (Dumfriesshire) is not the best preserved of medieval castles in Scotland. No towers survive, and no battlements which the imagination can people with men-at-arms, resplendent in livery. It does not even have dungeons with dripping walls, where one can listen half-expecting the squeak of medieval rats, or a great hall in which to re-create banquets in flickering rush-light. Yet Lochmaben Castle, amid leafy trees which give shelter on summer afternoons to hordes of picnickers, once played a vital role in Scotland's fight for freedom from English oppression.

Although a royal burgh, Lochmaben is now only a village, no larger than it would have been in the Middle Ages. Only a statue in the town centre and a café which proudly proclaims itself to be the 'Bruce Café' reveals that this was the home town of Robert the Bruce, the liberator of Scotland. Today golfers saunter in the shadow of the great earthen motte-hill or castle mound whereon once stood the castle of the Bruce family, and not far away, on its wooded promontory in Lochmaben Loch, stands the stone castle that replaced it.

In front of the stone castle are a series of mighty earthworks under which archaeology suggests that Edward I, the *Malleus Scottorum* (Hammer of the Scots), built one of the timber palisade forts (peels) that were a feature of his Scottish campaigns. It is not difficult to reconstruct Lochmaben Peel in the mind's eye. Defended with wide ditches and banks, it would have looked similar to the forts of the American Civil War, and only the tents pitched inside with their colourful banners and the armoured soldiery would betray their medieval date. Peels were the brain-child of Master James of St George, a brilliant Savoyard architect who had proved his worth to Edward I by designing and supervising the construction of such architectural masterpieces as Caernarvon and Conway Castles, in Wales.

As the fortunes of war changed, so did the ownership of Lochmaben Castle. Sometimes it was held by the English, sometimes by the Scots. Finally, in 1385, the castle passed for ever into Scottish hands and later kings embellished it as a royal residence.

But to fight for its independence, Scotland first had to have unity: this had been provided around 843, when Kenneth mac Alpin, king of the Scots, united his people with the Picts. During the next two centuries the rest of Scotland was gradually welded into a kingdom approximating to that of the modern country.

Duncan I was the first king of Scotland and his murderer, Macbeth, who came to the throne in 1040, did much to open up his kingdom to outside influences. His successor, Malcolm Canmore, continued this policy, having spent a year of Macbeth's reign in exile at the court of Edward the Confessor. His second wife, Margaret, was a Saxon princess, under whose influence Scotland became a refuge for all who hated William the Conqueror. The Normans could not leave this unchallenged and conducted a brief campaign ending with Malcolm being forced to swear fealty to William. The first step had been taken in the feudalisation of Scotland, a process which was to bring the country out of its long centuries of Iron-Age barbarism into the mainstream of European civilisation.

The process of feudalisation reached its peak in the reign of David I (1124-53). David had passed much of his youth in England, and through his English wife controlled considerable estates there. Unlike his predecessors he was not a vassal of the English king, and spent much of his time endeavouring to annexe territory in the north of England. He was, however, a great admirer of Norman ways, and introduced the Norman system of central and local government and various Anglo-Norman institutions. He settled estates in Scotland, and key positions in church and administration, upon many Anglo-Norman lords whom he had brought with him. In place of the old social system, which depended on individual loyalty to family and family head, a new system was instituted which depended on the tenure of land: with every grant of land went certain rights over the tenants who lived on it.

David I's pro-Norman policy had other far-reaching effects. His economic policy brought about the establishment of a series of burghs—towns with special trading rights—that led to a boom in Scottish imports and exports. To facilitate such a trade good coinage was necessary, and David introduced a monetary system modelled on the Norman penny. His religious beliefs led to the foundation of a series of abbeys, many of them daughter houses of English establishments, and to the spread of Norman architecture which was to be seen in ecclesiastical buildings from cathedrals to parish churches. The feudal system gave rise to the spread of villages of English type in the Scottish lowlands. The new feudal lords needed castles, and the first phase of castle building in Scotland can be attributed to this reign.

VISIBLE REMAINS

The remains of medieval Scotland are among the most romantic ruins in the country. Stark and forbidding castles speak more clearly than words of bitter feuds and bloodshed, while the gentle, crumbling walls of abbeys amid green lawns and flowers reflect the civilising effect of the Church. If castles and abbeys are the most evocative remains, one must not overlook the others, the simple parish churches, the bridges, the occasional market cross which provides a weathered focus for many a small town, speaking of times when such communities had not been outstripped by the mercantile boom of later centuries. Of the villages little remains except the low grassy mounds in fields to show that peasants once returned here after a long day's toil in the fields; nor do many visible remains of the medieval burghs survive as tokens of their prosperity, though the ancient street plans survive, preserving something of the old character beneath an overlay of sixteenth-century and later development.

Castles

The castle was the most conspicuous symbol of Scottish feudalism. As in England, the earliest castles were simple ringworks—earthen ramparts with an outer quarry-ditch, probably furnished with a timber gatehouse and timber breastworks, and enclosing various subsidiary timber buildings.

Far more abundant are the mottes—earth mounds sometimes with an encircling ditch or set within a subsidiary earthwork enclosure known as a bailey. There are well over two hundred mottes in Scotland, with a particularly dense distribution south of the Forth–Clyde line, but with some as far north as Sutherland.

Mottes seem to have been developed in England in response to the Norman Conquest, and excavation suggests that the surviving earthen mounds were stabilisers for rectangular timber towers. One of the few excavated mounds in Scotland, the Motte of Urr in the Stewartry of Kirkcudbright, was revetted by a clay facing on which the tower stood. The Mote of Urr itself is over 30ft (9·1m) high and 85ft (26m) in diameter, and is set within a 5½-acre bailey. There is a ditch round both motte and bailey. Today the earthworks are softened by the hand of time and carpeted with a covering of grass, and it is easy to forget that originally they were ugly weals on the landscape, mounds of raw earth crowned by functional timber towers, as architecturally displeasing as a Nissen hut, a savage military reminder to the local peasantry that steel dictated the terms by which they lived.

Such mottes remained in use for a very long time. Some may have been built as early as the time of Alexander I (1107–1124), while finds from sites such as the Motte of Hawick (Roxburghshire) show that some were still in use in the fourteenth century.

While motte-and-bailey castles were being built, stone castles were making their appearance in Scotland. The earliest are simple structures consisting of an enclosure wall defending a courtyard, in which ranges of stone, or more often timber, buildings were constructed. Some of these 'shell keeps' as they are called were stone replacements for the timber palisade round the tower of the larger mottes. Two fine examples can be

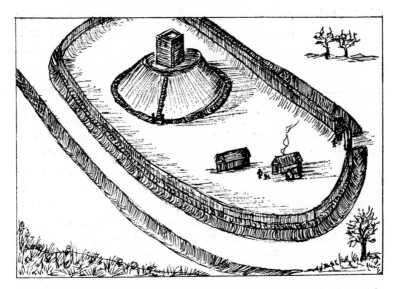

Fig 11 Reconstruction of the motte at Mote of Urr, Kirkcudbright, in the twelfth century

seen at the Doune of Invernochty (Inverness) and at the Peel Ring of Lumphanan (Aberdeenshire), where Macbeth made his last stand. Edward I may have fortified Lumphanan on his northern campaigns. The stone curtain-wall is now reduced to a bank except where the diligence of cattle has cleared back the vegetation to reveal cyclopean blocks resembling the handiwork of a Neolithic mason.

The finest and most 'romantic' of Scottish castles are those built during the Scottish Wars of Independence in the later thirteenth and early fourteenth century. This was one of the most dramatic periods in Scottish history. Alexander III mysteriously rode his horse over a cliff at Kinghorn, Fife, in 1286—the spot is now marked by an inscription seldom noticed by the streams of holiday traffic going to Burntisland—and he left no successor. The most obvious choice to follow him, the 'Maid of Norway', died on the journey over, and through the machinations of Edward I of England a puppet king, John Baliol (Toom Tabbard—'Empty Gown'), was set up. At the first opportunity Edward seized the chance to march on Scotland, with the intention of annexing it, and there began a bitter war in which the great national hero, William Wallace, played a stirring part. Wallace has left his mark in Scottish folklore throughout the land—bridges he crossed and caves in which he hid from the English are often pointed out. Only in Lanark, however, are there sites genuinely associated with him, for here the patriot struck the first blow of Scottish resistance. The church of St Kentigern, where he married Marion Braidfute (Broadfoot), still stands outside the town, its splendid thirteenth-century arches open to the sky, while the site of the castle of the English governor, Haselryg, is now a bowling green. A plaque marks the traditional site of Wallace's house in the Castlegate where his wife was burned alive by the English. A cave, long associated with him in the spectacular Cartland Crags on the nearby Clyde, could be visited by the intrepid until a few years ago when it became too dangerous. Each year on Lanimer Day the statue of Wallace in front of the parish church is adorned with a garland of flowers. It is the work of a self-taught sculptor in the nineteenth century. With its helmet, reminiscent of an Air Raid Precautions hat, it is folk art appropriate to a folk hero.

Edward died before his work was completed. His son, Edward II, was not the soldier his father had been and Bruce won the crown by his overwhelming victory at Bannockburn in 1314.

The great Scottish castles of the thirteenth and fourteenth centuries were built in response to improved techniques of siege warfare. They employ a high curtain-wall enclosing a courtyard or courtyards, with towers including a keep or *donjon*, an elaborate gatehouse and often an outer courtyard (the outer ward or bailey). Most of Edward's first castles in Scotland were peels like Lochmaben, and are known at places such as Linlithgow (West Lothian) and Kildrummy (Aberdeenshire). At Kildrummy a fine gatehouse was added by Master James of St George to the curtain-wall castle, but otherwise there are few remains in stone that can positively be ascribed to Edward's masons in Scotland.

Many castles of the Wars of Independence are outstanding: Rothesay (on Bute) which is circular; Caerlaverock (Dumfriesshire) which is triangular; and Bothwell (Lanarkshire) which is polygonal. Caerlaverock, with its fifteenth-century additions, has fairytale charm. Within its broad moat on which swans swim, it is situated in a particularly delightful corner of south-west Scotland. Nearby are the treacherous Solway mudflats which no doubt gave it added protection. The name means the 'fort of the lark's nest' and in contrast to many castles we have much information about Caerlaverock from archaeology and documentation. One of the most stirring events in its history was its siege by Edward I in 1300, described in a French poem. The poetic description of the castle as it was then could almost be taken from a present-day guidebook; only the men-at-arms are missing and where the timber drawbridge once was is now an immovable wooden bridge. Archaeologists found the remains of several medieval bridges when they cleared out the moat about twenty years ago. The French poet was of the view that, 'You will never see a more finely situated castle, for on the one side can be seen the Irish Sea, towards the west, and to the north the fair moorland, surrounded by an arm of the sea.' He justifiably likened its plan to that of a shield.

Until the fourteenth century Scottish and English castle architecture had many features in common, but at this time the distinctive tower house was developed, which endured with various modifications until the seventeenth century. In essence a tower house was a keep, with store rooms on the ground floor, a hall at first-floor level, and a private apartment for the lord on the third floor. For safety reasons the entrance was at first-floor level, approached by a ladder, and the ground floor was reached from the hall. Outside the tower was a small courtyard, known as a 'barmkin'.

An exceptionally emotive tower house was built at Threave on an island in the Dee in the Stewartry of Kirkcudbright. Visitors ring a bell on the bank for a ferry boat, and are rowed past the swans to the island. The long walk from the car park adds to the setting and gives the visitor a dramatic taste of life in the Middle Ages.

The later Scottish castles are variants of the tower house. It was not long before the occupants found it inconvenient to have three, or sometimes four floors, each consisting of one room approached by a circular or turnpike stair. So that no defensive advantage would be lost, additional rooms were constructed within the thickness of the walls. In the fifteenth century this trend reached its peak in castles such as Elphinstone Tower (Midlothian) or Cardoness Castle (Kirkcudbright), which have a maze of intra-mural chambers. An alternative solution was the addition of a wing or jam for private apartments on the long side. This produced L-plan tower houses, such as Craigmillar (Midlothian) or Aflleck (Angus), built at the end of the fourteenth century. The use of the L-plan meant that the doorway could be put at ground-floor level, at an angle between the jam and main building, where it was protected by cross-fire from the jam.

Churches and Cathedrals

David I reorganised bishops' sees in Scotland, establishing ten dioceses, an eleventh being formed at the end of the twelfth century when Lismore was separated from Dunkeld. In the fifteenth century Whithorn and Orkney were added when they became detached from York and Trondheim, and it is to the later Middle Ages that most of the Scottish cathedrals belong, though some early work can be seen in a few places.

Among the earliest is the tower of St Regulus (St Rule) in St Andrews, which originally belonged to the monastic cathedral of the Augustinian canons. All that now survives of this building is the tower and a choir. The tower is unusual in showing the apparent survival of Anglo-Saxon architectural techniques, employing as it does round-headed, two-light windows, with arches formed with single stones. There is little doubt, however, that it was built in the twelfth century, probably by masons from Wharram-le-Street in Yorkshire. The tower is reputedly haunted by a monk who, unlike many spectres, puts in regular appearances on the tower stairs during the opening hours of the monument. Lingering Anglo-Saxon styles of building can be seen far from their origins in the early cathedral on Birsay (Orkney). Now extensively ruined, it was built by the Norse Earl Thorfinn around 1050, and has a double-splay window of Anglo-Saxon type in the north wall of the nave.

The earliest widespread order of architecture in Scotland is the Romanesque—what in England would be termed Norman. It is characterised by round-headed arches for both doors and windows, neat, coursed masonry and plain, round columns with a base moulding set on a plinth. Columns and mouldings are decorated with geometric ornament, such as diamonds, dog's-tooth patterns (zigzags) and step patterns. The Scottish cathedral which shows this at its best is St Magnus' (Orkney) which replaced the cathedral on Birsay in the twelfth century and which was the work of English masons from Durham. Good Romanesque work can be seen on the cathedral at Dunfermline in Fife (where Robert the Bruce's heart is buried) and St Andrews.

The great age of cathedral building was the thirteenth century, when a wave of piety led to the construction of some outstanding achievements of Gothic architecture in Europe, such as the cathedrals of Notre Dame in Paris or Wells, Lincoln and Salisbury. Round-headed arches were replaced by pointed Gothic arches, initially slender and plain ('first pointed') later more ornate. Octagonal as well as round columns became popular, and subsidiary columns or shafts were often grouped around the main column.

The finest Scottish cathedrals of this period are Glasgow, Dunblane and Elgin. Of these Glasgow is the most complete, and is still in use. This remarkable edifice owes its design to the shrine of St Kentigern. It replaced a twelfth-century stone predecessor, and an ambulatory was provided around the building for pilgrims to the shrine, which was in a crypt under the eastern limb. The plan was unique to Scotland, but can be matched in Salisbury and Wells.

From the late thirteenth century Scottish ecclesiastical architecture diverges from the European mainstream. Occasional attempts to imitate current trends resulted, for example, in the east end of Melrose Abbey with its fine rose window perhaps ultimately inspired by somewhere such as Rheims. In general, however, Scottish builders developed their own particular style which employed round arches and drum columns after the manner of the Romanesque, as well as devices borrowed from secular architecture such as barrel vaults.

Several Scottish cathedrals which were rebuilt in the fifteenth and sixteenth centuries display these features: St Machar's in Aberdeen is a good example. To some extent the simplicity of the design was dictated by the intractable building qualities of Aberdeen granite and the buttressed walls have a corbelled and machicolated parapet that would not have looked out of place on a tower house.

The medieval parish churches reflect the same architectural traditions as the cathedrals. Apart from a number of very ruinous, or almost totally buried, chapels of simple, unicameral type, the earliest surviving churches in Scotland were built in the twelfth century. During this period Romanesque churches were erected in various parts of the country, most notably in the south-east, where one of the best-preserved examples is at Dalmeny (West Lothian). In contrast to the English, the Scottish Romanesque churches tend to be very plain, with almost no architectural detail. They are normally composed of an oblong nave with a small square-ended chancel, and are furnished with tiny, deeply splayed windows. Originally they had thatched or shingled timber roofs, and were probably whitewashed inside. Few display much carved detail. Dalmeny has a western tower and apsidal-ended choir and displays some carving on the doorway of the nave and on the arches separating the divisions of the church. At Leuchars (Fife) the outer walls of the choir and apse have richly ornamented double tiers of blank arcading. Concurrently with these larger parish churches simple chapels were built— St Margaret's chapel in Edinburgh Castle is a late twelfth-century example, erroneously associated with the wife of Malcolm Canmore.

Most parish churches of the thirteenth and fourteenth centuries survive without aisles, towers or transepts, and comprise simply an elongated rectangle divided into nave and chancel with a timber screen: a well-preserved example can be seen at Barevan (Nairnshire).

During the fifteenth and sixteenth centuries there was a revival of church building, and many earlier structures were more elaborately replaced. The parish church of Edinburgh, now St Giles Cathedral, was one of these, and still retains, from the fifteenth century, its attractive openwork crown of masonry. Such crowns, now vanished, adorned the churches of Dundee and Linlithgow, while a similar crown can still be seen at King's College, Aberdeen. Although its crown has now been replaced with a crown of thorns by Sir Basil Spence, the church of St Michael's, near Linlithgow Palace, remains one of the finest examples of Scottish late-medieval church architecture. The graceful and tall proportions of St Mary's, Haddington (East Lothian), have recently been admirably restored.

One medieval church deserves far more praise than it usually receives. This is Roslin chapel, which lies in the Pentland Hills less than half an hour's car journey from the centre of Edinburgh, in the village of Roslin. Generations of august visitors have marvelled at Roslin: Dorothy Wordsworth recorded in her diary that it was 'exquisitely beautiful', and Queen Victoria was so impressed with it that she 'expressed the desire that so unique a gem should be preserved to the country'. A unique gem it is. The wealth of carving inside is astonishing. It was begun in the mid-fifteenth century and finished within about forty years. Each column is different, and a wealth of fable is preserved in the stone carvings that adorn virtually every surface—Virtues and Vices, scenes from Scandinavian mythology, Bible stories, the dance of death and various other themes are represented. The most famous piece of sculpture, however, is the Prentice Pillar, a column 8ft high, of exceptionally fine workmanship. Stories abound concerning this pillar. One legend states that the Holy Grail is embedded in it, and some years ago tests with metal detectors indicated that there was indeed metal in the core of the column! More likely to be founded in truth, however, is the story of the apprentice who carved it. Legend tells that the master mason had received a pattern for a column from his patron, which was to be based on one in Rome. Hesitant to copy it without seeing the original, he went on a pilgrimage there, and while he was away his apprentice had a dream of the completed column and set about carving it. On his return the master mason was so outraged that his pupil could produce something he was himself incapable of doing that he killed him with his mallet and, accordingly, the church had to be reconsecrated. Certainly reconsecration crosses can still be seen on the walls.

One important ecclesiastical trend left its mark in Scottish medieval church architecture. This was the process of the endowment of secular clergy by the rich nobility, the non-monastic communities so created being known as collegiate churches. The objective was to ensure that the clerics so endowed would celebrate mass daily for the souls of the founder and his family. Because of the troubled nature of life in Scotland in the later Middle Ages, many of these remarkable churches have features associated with military building, such as battlements, heavy vaults, pack-saddle roofs and crow-stepped gables. The most militaristic is the Preceptory Church of Torpichen (West Lothian), the principal church of the Scottish branch of the Knights of St John. At Lincluden (Dumfriesshire), the architectural detail is particularly fine and includes a superb, carved-stone screen and the richly adorned tomb of Margaret, daughter of Robert III.

Church adornments of note are relatively few in Scotland, but worth searching for—such as the series of three altar tombs (of the Douglas family) in St Bride's Church, Douglas (Lanarkshire). The church also has a remarkable sixteenth-century clock. Fragmentary wall paintings survive in a few churches, such as those at Guthrie and Fowlis Easter (Angus), while there is a fine collection of medieval tombstones in St Andrews. At St Machar's (Aberdeen) there is a good Tournai graveslab. In the Western Highlands the traditions of Dark-Age Celtic sculpture continued, and through the Middle Ages a rich school of sculpture flourished leaving a legacy of cross slabs and crosses. These, apart from interlace, have interesting details which shed light on everyday life in the medieval Highlands. One of the best collections can be seen at Kilberry Castle (Argyll) and there are other important collections at Inchkenneth and Kilmory Knap in the same county.

Abbeys

The abbeys of medieval Scotland are the most evocative remains of the period. The eremetic monasticism of Dark-Age Scotland (see p 65) was not the forerunner of medieval monasteries, which were an extension of Regular monasticism that followed a Rule or code (from the Latin *regula* meaning a rule). The earliest rule was formulated by St Benedict around AD 529 and set the pattern for later monastic life. The Benedictine Rule reached England before the Norman Conquest, and was followed by the great Saxon monasteries of Northumbria. In the Middle Ages the Benedictine Order of monks was formulated from which various groups disseminated; notably the Cluniac Order (which took its name from the Burgundian monastery of Cluny), which stressed strict

Plate 11 Provost Skene's House (Aberdeen). Sixteenth century

Plate 12 The Penicuik Jewels of Mary, Queen of Scots. The locket (top left) does not belong with the jewels, but is contemporary

central control and elaborate ceremonials, and the Tironesian Order (named after the monastery at Tiron, near Chartres in France), which represented an attempt instituted by a Benedictine monk, Bernard, to restore simplicity to the monastic way of life and to reinstate the importance of manual labour. The Tironesians favoured handicrafts as the ideal form of manual labour and as a result artisans were attracted to the Order. In Scotland Tironesian houses were relatively common, though by the later twelfth century they were commonly referred to simply as Benedictines. Another attempt at reform was that made by Robert, Abbot of Molesme around 1098, when he and a fellow English monk settled in the French woods round Citeaux and gathered a following of monks. The outcome of this move was a new 'reformed' Order of the Cistercians (named after Citeaux). Cistercian monks venerated poverty, and renounced art and learning as detrimental to the spiritual life. They stressed the importance of manual labour in the fields. It was a strict Order, Cistercian houses are stark even today and must have been uncomfortable and cheerless then, the only compensation being an austere, clean simplicity.

All the monasteries following the Rule of St Benedict were for cloistered monks who were not concerned with the outside world. An alternative was offered by the Augustinians and the Premonstratensians, both of whom were concerned with the world outside the monastery, and preached to lay congregations. The Augustinians renounced personal possessions and were celibate. The Premonstratensians were stricter. The Augustinians were known as 'black canons' and the Premonstratensians as 'white canons' from the colour of their habits.

All the above mentioned Orders were present in medieval Scotland, and the flowering of monasticism was concentrated in the twelfth and early thirteenth centuries. No new abbey was founded after Sweetheart (Dumfriesshire), in 1273, though additions to existing structures continued to be made until the Reformation. David I founded a dozen priories and abbeys, mainly of the Cistercian and Augustinian Orders, and by the Reformation there were in excess of a hundred monastic foundations in Scotland.

The layout of the monasteries varies according to the Order or the

F   93

dictates of the site, but broadly speaking all conform to a similar basic plan, with a church and ranges of other buildings grouped round a square cloister. The buildings included a chapter house or meeting place (where a chapter of the Bible was read), a refectory or dining-room, a kitchen, a warming-room (the only room in the monastery which was heated), a parlour (in which talking was allowed) and a dormitory. Beyond the main complex were isolated buildings such as an infirmary, the abbot's or prior's lodgings, a guest house and corrodiars' houses (apartments for aged beneficiaries of the monastery). Such an arrangement was already being formalised on the Continent in Carolingian times, and was developed in France into the form in which it is found in Britain around the twelfth century.

The Scottish abbeys are as architecturally accomplished as those in England or France, often displaying a wealth of carved detail or even, as in the case of Dryburgh (Roxburghshire), wall paintings. The most famous are the group of 'Border Abbeys'—Dryburgh, Jedburgh, Kelso and Melrose. Of these Kelso is notable for being mainly Romanesque, with a remarkable Carolingian type of church with transepts and a tower at both ends. Melrose displays particularly fine Scottish work of the late fourteenth century, having been rebuilt after its destruction by Richard II of England in 1385. The most picturesque, however, is Dryburgh, the last resting place of Sir Walter Scott and Field Marshal Earl Haig. It is everyone's idea of what a 'Gothick ruin' should look like, nestling in a secluded horseshoe bend of the beautiful river Tweed. The site is surrounded by trees which frame the softly coloured and smoothed, weathered ruins on the three gently terraced levels which rise to the majestic walls of the abbey church. In summer the sweet smell of syringa and cut grass enhance the air of tranquility which must have inspired one of Dryburgh's most famous monks, Ralph Strode, the poet and philosopher friend of Chaucer and Petrarch. Dryburgh has its own 'Gothick romance'—a lady who lived among the ruins in the eighteenth century, attended by her fairy helper whom she called Fatlips. Her lover had been killed in the Jacobite rebellion of 1745, and having sworn never to see the light again, she hid herself away in the dank vaults and avoided all human contact.

The best preserved of all the Scottish monasteries is that on the tiny island of Inchcolm in the Forth, where its isolation gives a greater insight into the original appearance of the claustral buildings than anywhere else.

Burghs

Before the reign of David I there were no towns as such in Scotland, though there may have been nucleated settlements at key places such as Edinburgh and Stirling. David I encouraged the growth of towns not only by giving charters of special trading rights to existing communities, but also by founding totally new communities—medieval 'new towns'. These, too, were awarded charters of similar trading rights. Barons and important churchmen were encouraged to found their own towns, and among the ecclesiastical burghs were Glasgow and St Andrews.

By 1214 30 royal burghs existed, while by 1500 there were 150. Many of the early foundations grew rapidly and are important centres today, such as Inverness, Dumfries, Dundee and Lanark. A few did not last long—Old Roxburgh, for instance, is now no more than a ruined castle and a large field near the Tweed, having been replaced by Kelso on the other side of the river. Standing on the gentle slope down to the river, it is difficult to imagine that here once stood a town—hardly a bump betrays the sites of houses, churches and other buildings mentioned in documentary sources. No finds of note have been ploughed up in the neighbourhood of this lost town—it is almost as though it never existed—and no archaeologist has ever put a spade into its turf. Old Roxburgh is unique, although a few other medieval burghs also failed to grow, such as Lochmaben in Dumfriesshire.

The medieval Scottish burghs generally could not boast a population of more than about 500 people, or in a few cases perhaps 1,000. Because so many were new foundations, the street-plans show deliberate layout, usually in the form of ribbon development along a high street. Houses were set end-on along the streets, with elongated yards or gardens behind them, of which the end walls or delimiting banks served as an ad hoc boundary for the burgh as a whole. Town walls were not built in medieval Scotland, though 'ports' or 'gaits' were put up to control traffic on the main streets. The only town gate actually surviving is the heavily restored West Port in St Andrews. The cathedral precinct wall in St Andrews served as a town wall, while in Edinburgh a wall was eventually built after the Scottish defeat at Flodden in 1513—sections of the Flodden Wall still survive.

No town buildings except churches survive from before the sixteenth century. The majority of town houses would have been entirely of timber—traces of these have been found in excavations at Dumbarton, Linlithgow and St Andrews, for instance. At St Andrews a timber-hall house of the thirteenth–fourteenth century was among the excavated remains. As yet very little archaeological work has been done in Scottish towns, but recent excavations in several cities and towns is beginning to shed light on the way of life of the town dwellers of medieval Scotland.

Villages

From the twelfth century onwards Scotland developed a pattern of rural settlement similar to that in Northern England. Nucleated villages sprang up, many of which were the centres of parishes and were linked with outlying settlements. Village and outlying settlements comprised a 'shire', which was centred administratively on the king, bishop, abbot or a great layman.

Cultivated land extended in a large area round the village, and separate holdings consisted of several 'rigs' scattered about the cultivated land, each person holding strips in various fields. Each villager, too, had rights to use adjacent meadow and common pasture, and areas of hill-grazing were exploited from summer shielings. In the thirteenth century the development of the wool trade reduced these hill pastures, as did the attempts of monasteries and large landowners to annex great areas of them. Most villages were grouped round the church and lord's residence, though later in the Middle Ages 'fermtouns' (farm townships), 'kirktouns' (church townships) and 'milntouns' (mill townships) can be recognised.

In many parts of the Lowlands there are the recognisable remains of deserted medieval villages. Unlike the situation in England, where desertion followed the Black Death and later Elizabethan land enclosures, many of these villages were not deserted until the eighteenth century, during the 'Improvements'.

Kirkconnel (Waterbeck, Dumfriesshire) is a deserted village, tucked away from any sign of twentieth-century building in the tangle of mossy trees and rhododendrons of a private estate. The first visible sign of Kirkconnel is a broken market cross, almost obscured by the undergrowth. A tiny graveyard is filled mostly with nineteenth-century gravestones grouped round a post-Reformation chapel. But the graveyard is on the site of one even older, and the chapel stands on the low mound of an earlier building. Amid the later tombstones lie two grave-slabs side by side, worn flat by the Solway rains. Tradition (and a Department of the Environment plate) relate that these are the graves of Fair Helen and her lover, whose tragic romance is narrated in a border ballad

> Oh would I be where Helen lies
> On fair Kirkconnel Lea . . .

The story and the tombstone probably belong to the sixteenth century, shortly before the village was abandoned, and the fable is one of passionate murder and remorseful suicide, so beloved of folklore the world over.

The village proper lies clear of the trees in a wide meadow which dips down in a natural river terrace to the Kirtle Water. Excavations on the site showed that people built a timber hall there in the sixth or seventh century, but the village seems to have been left unoccupied until perhaps the fourteenth century, when flimsy timber houses were constructed on cobbled footings.

Very little is known archaeologically about these villages. Excavations on a few sites, however, have uncovered remains of 'longhouses'. These were common in England and consisted of a long building with dwelling-room and byre under the same roof alignment. Such longhouses were still in use in Scotland in the seventeenth and eighteenth centuries in the Lowlands, and even later in the Highlands. Probably most of the peasant dwellings were of timber or wattle and daub. The longhouse probably spread to the Highlands from the Lowlands, though no

8

MARY, QUEEN OF SCOTS, TO BONNIE PRINCE CHARLIE

The Scotland of Mary, Queen of Scots, was a land of sharp contrasts and of change. In many respects it was still medieval and, from the accounts of early travellers and indeed from the contemporary records of the Scots themselves, the standards of living appear to have been higher in Neolithic Skara Brae than in the hovels of Mary's peasants. Even in the capital city of Edinburgh in the time of her son, James VI and I, the Privy Council found it impossible to persuade the magistrates to take action to prevent the streets of the city being 'overlaid and coverit with middingis and the filthe and excrementis of man and beast'. Slightly earlier, after a visit to Scotland, Aeneas Sylvius (Pope Pius II) felt that he was returning to civilisation when he beheld Newcastle, having been horrified alike by the squalor of the Scots and the absence of morals among Scottish ladies. Where roads existed they were little better than tracks, though bridges were fairly common and well built, and the land was rendered difficult of traverse by forest, bog and moor. The Western Highlands and Islands were virtually a separate kingdom ruled by the Lords of the Isles, over whom the Scottish monarch had little control, while the constantly feuding Lowlands were the victims of wild, border raiders and such legendary brigands as the cannibal family of Sawnie Bean.

Against this depressing backdrop the Renaissance sophistication of Linlithgow and Falkland Palaces or the Great Hall at Stirling Castle strikes an odd note.

Plate 13 (above) Painted ceiling (Delgatie Castle, Aberdeenshire). Sixteenth century; (below) Culross (Fife). A typical seventeenth-century Scottish burgh

Plate 14 Craigievar Castle (Aberdeenshire), finished 1626. A late survival of the medieval tower house

Plate 15 Holyrood Palace (Edinburgh)

Plate 16 (above) Hopetoun House (West Lothian); (below) New Lanark, from a print of 1828

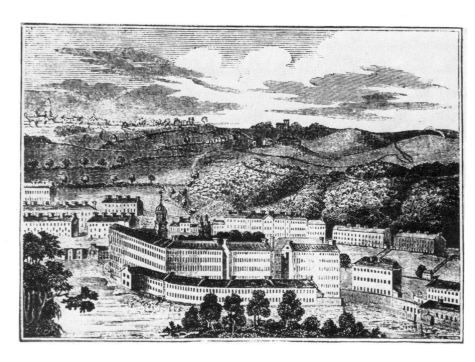

VISIBLE REMAINS

The visible remains of the sixteenth and seventeenth centuries in Scotland are very varied. The oldest town buildings that survive date from this period, as do several notable palaces. Architecture generally differs greatly, for medieval tower houses and medieval-style churches continued to be built alongside Renaissance houses, while many older castles were given a facelift with the addition of ornate new ranges. Some bridges, market crosses and other town structures (such as the city wall of Edinburgh), also belong to this period.

Castles and Palaces

By the fifteenth century in Scotland castles were commonly planned with a great hall and various other domestic buildings ranged about a central courtyard, a layout with an origin in the bailey-planning of the castles of enceinte. This design was taken up in the great Scottish palaces, which gradually lost the characteristics of their military origins and became domestic in appearance.

The earliest courtyard castle crowns a hill above a loch at Linlithgow (West Lothian). The site occupied by the later palace had been that of Edward I's peel, which had been replaced with a stone structure by James I, begun around 1425. The palace, however, owes its present plan to James V, who was born there and who converted it into a quadrangular building focussed on a central courtyard. Mary of Guise described it as the most princely home she had ever looked on. Much of the work, in fact, was the responsibility of a French master mason, though the general effect was Scottish. James V had a richly sculptured fountain placed in the central court, a copy of which stands at Holyrood House. The fountain flowed with wine for a visit of Bonnie Prince Charlie to Linlithgow in 1745. The palace was completed by James VI, who constructed a new frontage for the north range between 1618 and 1620, an exceptional example of Scottish Renaissance architecture. It was in Linlithgow Palace that Margaret, wife of James IV, awaited news of the disaster at Flodden, and where Mary, Queen of Scots, was born.

The building of Linlithgow Palace was in progress while the Great Hall at Stirling Castle was being erected by James III who died in 1488. This magnificent building, which has recently been undergoing renovation, represents the last and perhaps the finest flourish of medieval Gothic architecture in Scotland. Essentially a medieval hall with hammer-beam roof, it was compared in the eighteenth century with Richard II's Hall at Westminster, and described by Daniel Defoe as 'the noblest I ever saw in Europe'.

On another side of the quadrangle on to which the Hall faces is the palace block of James V. Although medieval in conception, it is a work of the Renaissance in detail, furnished with sculptures in true Renaissance style on baluster wall shafts with relief foliage. In keeping with Renaissance traditions, the figures are inspired by classical models, but their treatment is essentially native. To this period, too (*c* 1540), belong the Stirling heads, a superb series of fifty-six, oak, portrait roundels set into the wooden ceiling of the king's presence chamber, as well as the Chapel Royal, built in 1594 and entered through a classical doorway with Doric columns. In this courtyard can be seen the happy marriage of medieval and Renaissance, welded together, almost certainly, through the skill of French masons.

The finest flowering of early Renaissance architecture in Scotland can be seen in Falkland Palace, where French masons carried out intensive work between 1537 and 1541. Falkland, like Linlithgow, displays work of more than one period, but the courtyard façade of the south range with its buttresses and sculptures is its chief contribution to the Scottish Renaissance.

To the time of James IV belongs the oldest part of Holyrood House in Edinburgh, and the Great Hall of Edinburgh Castle. This early Renaissance taste patronised by the kings James IV and V bred no successors, until the end of the century, when a façade of faceted stonework was put up at Crichton Castle (Midlothian), directly inspired by Italian work such as the Palazzo dei Diamanti at Ferrara. Built between 1581 and 1591, it is a bizarre testimony to the taste of the earl of Bothwell.

Nobler and less unusual to the modern eye, the fine façade of the east range of Caerlaverock Castle (Dumfriesshire), built in 1638, epitomises the early classical Renaissance in Scotland. The magnificent Renaissance work in the Earl's Palace in Kirkwall, built around 1600 for Earl Patrick Stewart, is gracefully laid out round three sides of a square and furnished with a notable series of oriel windows, corbelled out from the wall.

Tower Houses

While the Renaissance leavened the palaces of kings, medieval castellated architecture lumbered into the sixteenth century as the bleak and forbidding tower houses of the lairds. Sixteenth- and early seventeenth-century tower houses are most abundant in the Lowlands where Border troubles and the threat of invasion from England made them a still functional form of defence.

The old-fashioned, L-plan towers were elaborated by setting the wings or jams diagonally to the main towers, to provide covering fire for the main building. From here it was a short step to the addition of a second jam at an opposite corner, to give total covering fire, and these Z-plan castles became very popular in the sixteenth century, particularly in north-east Scotland. Sometimes the towers were round, rather than square, as at Claypotts (Angus), built between 1569 and 1588, or Muness Castle (on Unst in Shetland), the most northerly castle in Britain. Square towers, however, continued to be used, as at Glenbuchat (Aberdeenshire).

Although no military improvement was made on the Z-plan, tower houses underwent some external changes in the late sixteenth century, when a style known as the 'Scottish baronial' developed. The gaunt, rectangular towers were enlivened with turrets, crow-stepped gables and corbelling. The most famous example of the style is undoubtedly Glamis, with its 'fairy tale' charm. Midmar (Aberdeenshire), built around 1570, is less famous but notable. The tradition carried on into the seventeenth century, and can be seen at its best in Craigievar Castle (Aberdeenshire), built in 1626, which is a modified L-plan house set within a barmkin with angle towers. It stands today complete and without later additions in an attractive Highland setting.

During the later sixteenth and seventeenth centuries the tower-house homes of small landowners or lairds quickly lost their militaristic character. From structures such as the Castle of Park (Wigtownshire), built in 1590, houses without parapets and fewer angle turrets evolved. They were increasingly enriched inside and out with Renaissance detail. Windows were made larger, gunloops became fewer, window glass became common and, inside, the rooms were ornamented with fine wood-carving, wrought ironwork and painting on plaster, canvas or timber panels. The painted ceilings to be seen in Scottish homes of the sixteenth or early seventeenth century are a distinctive Caledonian contribution to the history of interior decoration. Executed on flat boards, the paintings display a rich assortment of medieval and Renaissance motifs and armorial designs, the subjects sometimes taken from imported pattern books, but always given an unmistakable character and rustic charm. Such painted ceilings were to be found in churches, palaces and town houses—there is a good example in the Abbey Strand near Holyrood House in Edinburgh—but many of the best are in laird's houses. When plaster ceilings became fashionable, from the early eighteenth century onwards, these were frequently covered up—which has resulted in their fortunate preservation.

Towns

As elsewhere in Europe, the sixteenth and seventeenth centuries were a period of town growth in Scotland. Edinburgh, Dundee, Aberdeen, Perth, Glasgow and St Andrews were the six main burghs, though, until the rise of the tobacco lords in the eighteenth century, Glasgow was little more than a large village, and the other burghs hardly any larger. A population of 2,000 represented a sizeable burgh—Stirling and Ayr, next in importance to St Andrews, had populations of around this figure in 1600, while many of the smaller burghs supported a population of only a few hundred people. The entire population of Scotland in the time of James VI was probably about 850,000—just over twice that of modern Edinburgh. Most of the trade was concentrated in the east-coast burghs. Fife was described by James VI as 'a beggar's mantle with a fringe of gold', and ports such as Dundee and Aberdeen exported small quantities of wool, skins, smoked and dried fish and coarse cloth and imported iron, timber, pitch, tar, wine, fine cloth and some luxury goods. Most of the trade was conducted with the Low Countries and the Baltic.

Within the burghs stone-building gradually replaced the use of wood, with an intermediary stage of part timber, part stone, houses. Very few town buildings, however, survive from the sixteenth century. One of the most famous is John Knox's House in Edinburgh High Street, which almost certainly had no connection with the fiery preacher. Its present form is late sixteenth-century work, and it had timber galleries which projected from the south front at first and second-floor levels. Timber frontages were commonplace, affording a continuous covered passage at ground-floor level and open or enclosed galleries supported on posts at first- and second-floor levels. The upper floors were often corbelled out over the street, and can still be seen in Edinburgh in the Canongate, for example in Huntly House or Moray House. By the seventeenth century the timber posts of the ground-floor arcade were being replaced by stone piers, which provided a pedestrian arcade for passers-by. Gladstone's Land, in Edinburgh, is a good example of this, dating from around 1630. Such partly-timber houses were almost as great a fire-risk as their all-timber predecessors, and gradually all-stone building became the norm.

At Culross (Fife) chance has preserved a seventeenth-century burgh almost unaltered. The stone buildings are enlivened by harling, the Caledonian equivalent of roughcast, and much of the burgh is now in the care of the National Trust for Scotland. Culross flourished through trade with the Low Countries, and its wealth was augmented by coal-mining. Even in the time of James VI it boasted a coalmine that ran out under the sea—one of the wonders of its day. Most of the houses are two or three storeys high, with typical Scottish crow-stepped gables. Gay, pantiled roofs and windows, glazed on the upper part and shuttered on the lower, were perhaps of Flemish inspiration. In the early seventeenth century the leading citizen of Culross was Sir George Bruce, and his palace, built between 1597 and 1611, boasts some of the finest painted ceilings in Scotland as well as a charming garden. Kirkwall

(Orkney) also preserves something of its seventeenth-century character.

Most of the surviving houses were the residences of wealthy merchants or craftsmen. A few town houses belonged to the nobility or important churchmen who required a town residence. Many of these survive in Edinburgh, but there are others in the provinces, among which Mar's Lodging (Stirling) is an outstanding example.

Churches

Church building declined after the Scottish Reformation. The majority of post-Reformation kirks were simple, unicameral buildings, as the old divisions into nave and chancel were felt to be a hindrance to proper congregational worship. Gothic styles of architecture persisted, as for example at Lyne (Peeblesshire), where richly traceried Gothic windows adorn a building erected between 1640 and 1645. From the simple rectangle evolved a T-shaped plan; a projecting wing housing the laird's burial vault and loft. The need for such a construction arose from the custom of building a laird's loft to house the laird and his family, often above a family vault and approached by its own stair, rather after the fashion of a box at the theatre. Some were furnished with with-drawing-rooms, in which refreshment could be taken between services, or a lavatory. A particularly good example of this phenomenon can be observed in the delightful little church at Abercorn (Midlothian). Other churches had a cruciform (usually Greek Cross) plan. Lauder church (Berwickshire), designed in 1673 by Sir William Bruce, is a very fine example of this type.

The Countryside

No great changes occurred in the sixteenth and seventeenth centuries. Oats and bere were grown, using an infield-outfield system of cultivation; the infield was farmed for about four years until the yield was too poor to be worth harvesting, then allowed to lie fallow for a similar period in favour of the outfield. The Elizabethan enclosure movement did not have any effect on Scotland, and the ox-plough was still used to till the rigs, wastefully separated by ditches or banks. Rig-and-furrow traces can still be seen in most parts of Scotland, including hillsides which were favoured because of their natural drainage.

Because of the later eighteenth-century 'Improvements' in the Lowlands, there are very few peasant dwellings in Scotland that pre-date about 1750, though it can be inferred from the accounts of early travellers and from excavation that the medieval type of longhouse and shieling remained the basic house types up to the Improvements. One longhouse was excavated at John Brown's House in Muirkirk (Ayrshire) in the 1920s, and was found to have a stone-built foundation measuring 74ft × 20ft, with dwelling, byre and barn under the same roof alignment, and with a central hearth. It was occupied until the late eighteenth century. A smaller dwelling investigated at Lour (Stobo, Peeblesshire) had consisted of a storeroom next to a dwelling with an indoor midden and a hearth set off-centre. It formed part of a small township associated with a tower house, and was occupied in the seventeenth century. A description of a house in Ayrshire in 1811 states:

> the part of the building which served the family for lodging, sleeping, eating, dairying, was the 'inseat', about 12 to 14 feet square with a fire in the centre or at the gable, without jambs or smoke funnel. On large farms another apartment, the 'spense', held the meat chest, sowen tub, some beds, a cask to collect urine called the wash tub, spinning wheels and reels when not in use and the gudewife's press if she had one. The other part of the building was occupied by the cattle which generally entered the same door as the family.

Early travellers in Scotland were amazed at the low turf-built houses with a hide hung over a gap for a door and with sheep grazing on the roofs. Another account of Orcadian houses by a traveller in 1577 informs us that:

> their houses are verie simply builded with pibble stone, without any chimneys, the fire being in the middest thereof. The good man, wife, children and other of their familie eate and sleepe on the one side of the house and their catell on the other, very beastlie and rudely in respect of civilitie.

Dr Johnson's description of a Highland cottage, 'constructed with loose stones, ranged for the most part with some tendency to circularity', is clearly applicable to most of Scotland until the late eighteenth century, and to some parts even later.

Until the Improvements and the notorious Highland Clearances, which caused so much misery and resulted in the deserted villages that are such a sad feature of the Highland landscape today, the standard type of settlement was the clachan or baile—the farm township. These clusters of buildings of varying size, included long rectangular buildings, 50ft × 14ft, of true longhouse type, along with smaller structures, stack yards, corn-drying kilns and platforms of stone for the peat stack. The surviving remains, such as those excavated at Rosal and Lix in Perthshire, do not appear to pre-date the eighteenth century, and it is possible that stone was not used for Highland houses before this time.

Everyday Life

Castle inventories, such as that of Caerlaverock (Dumfriesshire), drawn up in the sixteenth and seventeenth centuries, show that the homes of the rich were well appointed, even if James VI found it necessary to send out begging letters to meet the costs incurred in preparing Holyrood House for his bride. 'Money is scarce in these parts,' he wrote—so scarce in fact that he had to borrow a pair of silken hose for himself from the earl of Mar.

The average merchant's house was furnished with wooden cupboards, settles, curtained beds, and a table, and the solar would have been hung with Arras. The doors from Mary of Guise's house, or from Amisfield Tower (Dumfries), the latter showing Samson and the lion and dating from 1660, show the expertise of the Scottish woodcarver. The accomplished Cathcart portrait heads were executed under French influence in the mid-sixteenth century, while a fine cupboard traditionally associated with Queen Mary (now in the National Museum in Edinburgh) has finely worked linenfold panels on the sides. Pottery continued in the medieval tradition, with large green-glazed jugs being the commonest products, alongside smaller pipkins or cooking pots, though cooking was still done in three-legged bronze cauldrons which remained fashionable until ousted by iron ones in the late eighteenth century. Wood continued to be used for most domestic vessels, including *quaichs*, the small wooden two-handled drinking bowls popular throughout Scotland—in the eighteenth century these had staves of alternate colours joined with feathered edges. Stoneware jugs with face masks, called Bellarmines, were imported from the Continent, and English pottery and glass vessels were sometimes used.

The medieval type of ring brooch continued to be produced into the sixteenth century, often with blundered charms derived from the '*IHESUS NAZARENUS REX IUADAEORUM*' (Jesus Christ, King of the Jews) of the medieval originals. A fine series of quoit-shaped brooches with richly chased ornament were executed in silver or brass, dating mainly from the seventeenth century. Slightly earlier, the Ballochyle and Kindrochit brooches display rock-crystal ornament.

The seventeenth century saw a revival of old traditions of Celtic art most surprisingly manifesting themselves on interlace-decorated powder horns produced in the north-east, while imported blades were turned into Scottish swords with the addition of a basket hilt, and fine ornament was used to decorate the butts of typically Scottish pistols.

Fig 12 Sixteenth-century silver brooch from Kindrochit Castle, Aberdeenshire

Highlanders in the seventeenth century carried targes—a type of round shield made of two circular pieces of wood, pegged cross-grained together and covered with leather which was tooled and set with studs.

The National Museum possesses one with applied silver ornament rather than studs, which belonged to Bonnie Prince Charlie. Such targes are similar to the shields carried by Pictish warriors on Dark-Age sculpture, and thus perhaps, the gap between the Dark Ages and the eighteenth century is bridged.

9

THE AGE OF INDUSTRY

New Lanark was one of the wonders of its age, a foretaste of better things to come for the workers of Britain. It is almost unchanged since the early nineteenth century, and though no longer a centre for textile production still serves industry under the management of the Gourock Rope Works. Its setting, a narrow plain on the bank of the Clyde near Lanark, is as unlike any industrial landscape one could imagine. It looks out on trees, and a short walk brings the visitor to Corra Linn, one of the most picturesque of the waterfalls of the Clyde. Here is the building that housed the first co-operative shop in Britain; not far off, on the opposite side of the street, is the imposing façade of Robert Owen's unusual school, the 'Institute for the Reformation of Character'.

New Lanark's story is a part of that of the Industrial Revolution itself. It began with a partnership between Richard Arkwright, the inventor of the water frame, and David Dale, a Glasgow merchant. Between them they selected the site of New Lanark for their enterprise, which they hoped would become a new Manchester, and factory and industrial housing were put up, the mills being in operation by 1786. Dale and Arkwright quarrelled, and under Dale's skilful direction the new mills prospered, making use of such major technological innovations as Crompton's spinning mule and Cartwright's power loom. The scene was set for New Lanark's most famous manager to take over—Robert Owen.

Owen arrived in New Lanark in 1798. By 1800 he had married Dale's daughter and was beginning his revolutionary experiments in factory management. David Dale had employed five- and six-year-old pauper children in his factory. Owen abandoned this practice, employing neither paupers nor children under ten, and set up a school, intended for both the young and old in his employ. He believed in music and dance as a relaxation from hard work—so much so that one of his ex-employees complained that he tired them out more with dancing than with working. To encourage productivity, Owen suspended a 'monitor' above each worker's head—a four-sided wooden block with its faces painted different colours. According to how hard they were working the cube was turned to display a different face—white meant excellently, black carelessly and indolently.

Thousands flocked to New Lanark to see the effects of Owen's amazing social and educational philosophy. Visitors included the Grand-Duke Nicholas of Russia, and between 1815 and 1825 no fewer than 20,000 people officially visited New Lanark. In less than a century Scotland had leaped forward into the modern age.

On the eve of the Jacobite rebellions Scotland had been largely feudal. In the Highlands the clan chiefs held sway like Iron-Age tribal leaders, administering justice and demanding total loyalty from their clansmen, who lived on a cultural level little improved since the Iron Age.

> The inhabitants stick close to their ancient and idle way of life; retain their barbarous customs and maxims; depend generally on their chiefs as their sovereign lords and masters; and being accustomed to the use of arms, and inured to hard living, are dangerous to the public peace.

So wrote Duncan Forbes of the Highlanders in 1745, and he could well have been describing their Caledonian ancestors. The situation was little better in the Lowlands, for here, outside the few towns, the lairds had similar feudal powers over their tenants and in town and country alike the vast majority of the population lived and died in abject poverty.

Politically, the aftermath of the Jacobite rebellions put an end to feudalism. Acts were passed by the Hanoverian parliament which not only forbade clansmen to carry weapons or wear tartan, but which in one blow ended the legal powers of the clan chiefs and lowland lairds, putting justice back in the courts. Like the Romans before them, the Hanoverians marched into the Highlands, opening up the glens with their forts, roads and bridges. But important though this was for communications, it did little for the economy, and the real revolution came not from the crown, but from the land and the people: the economic revolution of the eighteenth and nineteenth centuries dragged a feudal society into the industrial age.

In 1745, over half the population of Scotland was concentrated in the Highlands. A century later the situation was radically different. The resources of the Highlands did not permit rapid expansion and as the south prospered the north grew more and more impoverished. A boom in population (resulting from the introduction of the potato in the mid-eighteenth century) was met with the injustices of absentee landlords and the displacement of thousands when their lands were turned over to mass sheep farms.

The march towards an industrial Scotland began in the late seventeenth century with agricultural improvements and a resulting boom in trade. Technological developments in the eighteenth century in threshing, ploughing and farm equipment were added to the seventeenth-century improvements in livestock breeding and crop yields. Improved farming led to a population boom in general and the growth of towns and villages, which in turn led to keener trade and greater incentive for improved farming. The agrarian revolution paved the way for the industrial. The managers of big farming estates were responsible for estate mills and for the building of turnpike roads which facilitated the transport of raw materials and finished goods to and from factories. Cattle, grain and potatoes were exported, and cattle in particular required drove roads and further improvements in communications. The countryside too provided Scotland with some of her emergent industries —whisky distilleries grew out of illicit local stills, and the Scottish breweries, so important today, owe their origins to this period. Land reclamation, drainage, dyke-building and other estate activities led to quarrying, building and mining. Aristocratic landowners were at the forefront of such development, and there were good precedents behind the opening of a woollen mill by the Duke of Argyll at Inverary in 1775.

As the economy improved, so did overseas trade. Scotland became the major centre for the importing of tobacco and sugar, which gave rise to sugar refining, rum distilling and snuff manufacture. Soon cotton was added to the list of imports and most of this trade, with America and the West Indies, flowed through Glasgow and the west of Scotland. Glasgow grew rich on the tobacco trade. In the east, trade fostered links with the Baltic and the Low Countries (such links had existed since the Middle Ages), which in turn gave rise to other industries.

Textiles were the first concern of Scottish industry. The metal industries were not slow to develop, however, especially after the discovery of coke-smelting which was pioneered in the Carron works, opened in 1760. The 1780s were a period of great expansion in the iron industry, and by 1843 Scotland was producing 25 per cent of Britain's iron.

The effects of this boom were mixed. It led to all the evils of the factory system, to the growth of slums and slum housing, to the exploitation of the workers and to the rise of the capitalist merchant and industrialist class. It also led to the improvements, the rise in standards of rural life, to the building of fine country houses, and elegant urban terraces. It opened up Scotland to outside influences as never before, it improved communications and made the land not just an important part of Britain but an important part of the world.

VISIBLE REMAINS

Hardly a town or village in Scotland has not some buildings still surviving from this period which give much of the character to present-day Scotland. In burghs, old houses and municipal buildings of the sixteenth and seventeenth centuries were demolished and replaced. The story is well-exemplified by Lanark, which was almost totally rebuilt after 1823—'Such was the effect of this modern architecture that proprietors soon began to dilapidate their time-worn and hovel-looking mansions and to rear edifices which now display an air of elegance', wrote a local historian in 1828. Not long previously every house bar one in the town is recorded as being thatched, while a century later only one thatched house remained. Sometimes, as in Lanark, the old buildings remained, hidden behind new frontages. A photograph taken in Dundee in the late nineteenth century shows eighteenth-century cottage-style houses dwarfed by tenements built in front of them.

In the countryside, stately homes and cottages, drove roads and toll roads with their elegant toll houses, windmills and grassed-over remains of old ironworks abound.

Military Remains

The opening up of the Highlands by the Hanoverian army has left some fascinating remains in northern Scotland. Names like Fort Augustus and Fort George have a ring about them which recalls the Wild West, and indeed the Hanoverian soldiers must have felt something of the same sense of isolation in an alien land as did the American soldiers a century or more later.

Of all the Hanoverian military antiquities in Scotland, Fort George (Inverness) is still occupied by the army. It was begun in 1748, and can justifiably be regarded as one of the finest, late, artillery fortifications in Europe. Originally it accommodated about 200 men in its 16 acres.

Of the smaller defensive works, Ruthven Barracks (Inverness) was sacked by Bonnie Prince Charlie and never reoccupied. This bleak, isolated building was constructed in 1719 on the site of the castle of the lords of Badenoch. Two barrack blocks confront each other across a square courtyard.

Of the remaining military remains of the Jacobite period, one might single out Wade's bridge at Aberfeldy (Perthshire). It shows army architecture at its best, and its simple, elegant lines compare favourably with the more ambitious bridges of later times.

Country Mansions

It is in country mansions that the finest achievements of Scottish architecture can be seen which date from after the restoration of Charles II, and some of the finest examples of British architecture of the period can be seen in the work of a series of great Scottish architects like William Adam, Robert Adam and W. H. Playfair, who also achieved great fame south of the border.

There is an enormous diversity of design in Scottish country mansions, the finest of which are either classical or Gothic in style. Classical architecture had been revived at the Renaissance, and was to be given a further lease of life in the eighteenth century with the discovery of Pompeii, and with an upsurge of interest in classical antiquity fostered by the 'grand tour'—a tour of the Continent usually made by wealthy young men. This cultural pastime often served as an excuse for gentlemen to buy Greek and Roman antiquities with which to adorn their homes, as well as treasures looted from Etruscan tombs. Gothic architecture on the other hand stemmed not from a genuine interest in the medieval world (the word 'Gothic' was used by eighteenth-century observers to describe some of the finest medieval architecture because they regarded it as barbarous, like the work of the Goths), but from a romanticism which associated the Middle Ages with ruined abbeys, knights in armour and horror stories. The romantic Gothic revival was given a particular boost in England in the late eighteenth century by Horace Walpole, whose castellated home, Strawberry Hill, reflected the same taste for the bizarre that he showed in his mannered Gothic novel *The Castle of Otranto*. In Scotland, where medieval styles of architecture still endured in the seventeenth century, it is not always easy to say where traditional Gothic ends and neo-Gothic begins, a neo-Gothic that was to persist into Victorian times.

Of the great Scottish architects who designed country houses, the earliest of note was Sir William Bruce, whose greatest achievement was the remodelling of Holyrood House. Of all the country houses that he designed, by far the best is Hopetoun, built at Craigiehall not far from Edinburgh, for the first Earl of Hopetoun, between 1699 and 1702. As it stands today in its superbly landscaped grounds, Bruce's work is obscured by the enormous Adam façade and forecourt.

Hopetoun House as it is today is mainly the work of William Adam and his sons, and its fine interior boasts an outstanding collection of paintings, including works by Rubens, Titian, Tenniers and Gainsborough.

Of William Adam's major surviving works, the most arresting is Duff House (Banff), built in 1730 for William Duff. In contrast to most of the work that one associates with Adam, it is more baroque than classical in appearance, though the conventional plan of linking a main block to side pavilions with screen walls is quite in keeping with eighteenth-century style. Also impressive is the better-preserved Culzean Castle (Ayrshire), now in the custody of the National Trust for Scotland and open to the public. Built between 1777 and 1792, it has superb plaster ceilings, and can rightly claim to be one of the finest Georgian Gothic houses in Scotland. Its clifftop situation lends to the Gothic effect, and the luxuriant gardens befit the romantic image.

Burgh Architecture

Of the burgh architecture of the eighteenth and early nineteenth centuries, the greatest achievement was the new town of Edinburgh. Until the eighteenth century Edinburgh had grown more insalubrious and crowded along the narrow ridge which leads from the castle to Holyrood. Town expansion was necessary, and plans were laid and designs invited for a new town in 1766. The plan adopted for the new town was that proposed by James Craig, who devised Queen Street and St Andrews Square. The buildings of Craig's project show no uniformity of style and it was left to Robert Adam to introduce the device of treating entire blocks of buildings as units with uniform architecture. His models were the terraces of London and Bath, and he set the mood of subsequent new town development in Edinburgh with his masterly Charlotte Square. The town continued to grow in the early nineteenth century, to culminate with Playfair's Calton Hill terraces. The overall layout of Edinburgh was classical, and the classical image (which has earned it the name of the 'Athens of the North') is emphasised by the Temple folly which crowns Calton Hill itself.

Industrial Remains

The most interesting visible remains are perhaps those of ironworks, several of which are now derelict ruins. Among the saddest are those of Wilsontown (Lanarkshire), founded around 1780. The Wilsons, who gave their name to the works, went bankrupt in 1812, after having spent £100,000 on developing the site. The ruins of the engine house can still be seen, as well as other grassed-over remains, from which jagged fragments of masonry protrude. The ironworks are in a desolate setting, as indeed are the much better-preserved Bonawe works (Argyll), now in the care of the Department of the Environment. At Bonawe ironworking had begun as early as 1730, and both charcoal and peat were tried as fuel. The real history of the site, however, begins in the 1750s, and from then on charcoal ironworking continued on the site until 1866. The furnace still has its chimney, metal lintels and ruined casting house. Also preserved are a filling house and sheds for ore and charcoal, the ore being brought from Furness by sea. Contemporary with the ironworks is a block of tenements intended as housing for the workers, completed in 1759. Also of the charcoal smelting phase are the remains at Glenbuck (Ayrshire).

Modern coke smelting was first employed in the famous Carron works in 1759. Nothing survives of the original foundry, but in its day it made industrial history. James Watt experimented here with his steam engine before the Soho (Birmingham) factory was opened, and John Adam designed fireplaces which were cast at the Carron works. Its name has passed into English usage as 'carronade', the type of gun cast there which Nelson used on the *Victory*.

Everyday Life

The industrial revolution had its effect on the everyday life of Scotland. Brass, which had been used fairly universally for metal products up to the middle of the eighteenth century, by the nineteenth had been extensively replaced by iron. The three-legged brass cooking pots that had been popular since the Middle Ages were replaced by iron versions —so rapid was this changeover that when brass pots were found in mid-nineteenth-century excavations they were believed to be Roman. The traditional Scottish fare of oatcakes and bannocks continued to be made, now turned on iron bread-spades and baked on iron griddles.

Pewter continued for tableware, and increased in popularity. Although Scottish liquid measures had been abolished in 1707, the eighteenth-century Scots still liked good measure and employed the old units. Characteristic of the period is the 'tappit hen', the pint measure which actually measured three imperial pints. Scottish silverware of the eighteenth century graced the finest tables and was of very high quality, rivalling the contemporary English products.

Eighteenth-century Scottish women still fastened their plaid with circular brooches, usually of brass and up to 8in across. Some were love tokens, as were the Luckenbooth brooches, named after the Edinburgh jewellers' quarter near St Giles. These consisted of a single or double heart, sometimes crowned and cast in silver. Versions are still obtainable in Scottish jewellers' shops today.

EPILOGUE

There is one place in Scotland where it is possible to take in the entire panorama of her history in one sweep, the majestic hill known as Arthur's Seat which rises behind Holyrood House in Edinburgh.

Walk down the Canongate to the seventeenth-century posting inn, White Horse Close, and turn past Holyrood and the brewery to the gates that lead on to the lower slopes of Arthur's Seat. At once you are in the past. Sheep graze on either side of the road that leads up the hill, and a short walk takes you up under Salisbury Crags, themselves an awe-inspiring work of nature that is composed of some of the oldest rocks in the world. On the slopes of this hill have been found prehistoric stone implements dating back to the time of the first hunters, and bronze tools by the first metalsmiths. Follow the road round under the Craigs and you reach Dunsapie, a small Iron-Age hillfort. From here it is possible to look down at Duddingston Loch, where one of the most important late Bronze-Age hoards in Scotland was found, and to look up towards the summit of Arthur's Seat itself. Immediately in front of you are the grassy terraces of field systems, mostly dating from the Middle Ages. Follow them up to the summit, and you are back in the Dark Ages, for here, almost certainly, was a Dark-Age British fort. Pause for a moment to reflect that on the slopes below a Roman ring was recently found, then look at the panorama of Edinburgh before you. Here is the principal arena of Scottish history, where many great dramas were enacted. Finally, if the weather is clear, look out towards the Forth. In the distance you ought to see the two Forth bridges, the one a triumph of nineteenth-century technology, the other of twentieth-century engineering. Tomorrow they will be a part of ancient Scotland.

GAZETTEER

Over 300 monuments in Scotland in the guardianship of the Department of the Environment are open to the public and most of them are either tended by a custodian who can supply guidebooks and descriptive leaflets or have a descriptive plate explaining what can be seen. In addition to these, there are many more in the care of the National Trust for Scotland or in private ownership which are open to the public, usually for a small admission charge. Thousands of others are not laid out for the public and range from the impressive to the less well preserved.

The following gazetteer is a personal selection of sites which I feel are particularly worth visiting, and I have tried to include a representative selection of all the major visible classes of antiquities. My motives in selecting sites have been varied, and are based on what I feel the general visitor will find most interesting, not necessarily what is the most archaeologically significant. Factors such as accessibility, preservation and scenic value have been taken into consideration in making the selection, and thus one site may be included because it is easily accessible and typical, while another may have been selected because it has many unusual features and is in a particularly scenic setting.

The list is intended simply as a guide to sites which the visitor *may* like to visit; it is not intended to take the place of a map and a full gazetteer, from which he can assess how interesting or accessible the site is likely to be for him. Fortunately, there are many good gazetteers available. The most indispensable is *Scotland* (1970, 6th ed), the HMSO guide to ancient monuments, which describes all the sites in State care, how to get to them, and also has a useful introductory text. For prehistoric and Dark-Age monuments there are E. MacKie's *Scotland: an Archaeological Guide* (1975), and R. W. Feachem's *Prehistoric Scotland* (1963); while for Roman remains there is R. J. A. Wilson's *Guide to the Roman Remains in Britain* (1975). Industrial monuments are listed and described in J. Butt's *Industrial Archaeology of Scotland* (1967), while the main prehistoric and Roman monuments in southern Scotland are listed in J. Scott's *South-West Scotland* (1966) and A. & G. Ritchie's *South-East Scotland* (1972). The monuments in the Northern Isles appear in my own *Orkney and Shetland: an Archaeological Guide* (1974).

Inclusion of a site in the following gazetteer does not mean that there is a right of public access. Many are on private land and permission to visit them should first be sought from the landowner.

As a rough guide to the relative importance of the monuments a star rating has been employed; again this is a personal assessment.

★★★★ Major sites not to be missed if a visit is possible. Some are outstanding because of their archaeological importance and general preservation, others because they are the best preserved examples of their class.

★★★ Sites with unusually well preserved remains for their class of monument.

★★ Sites better preserved than average, of scenic merit, or exceptional interest.

★ Slightly better than average sites.

NEOLITHIC REMAINS (*c* 4500 BC–2000 BC)

SITE	COUNTY	RATING	GRID REF
Houses			
Skara Brae	Orkney	★★★★	HY 2318
Stanydale	Shetland	★	HU 2850
Ness of Gruting	Shetland	★	HU 2848
Isbister	Shetland	★	HU 5864
Chambered Tombs			
Brackley	Argyll	★★★	NR 7941
Crarae	Argyll	★★	NR 9897
Cairn Ban	Arran	★★	NR 9926
Torrylin	Arran	★	NR 9521

SITE	COUNTY	RATING	GRID REF
Camster, Grey Cairns	Caithness	****	ND 2644
Cairnholy I & II	Kirkcudbright	***	NX 5153
Steinacleit	Lewis	*	NB 3954
Unival	North Uist	**	NF 8066
Clettraval	North Uist	**	NF 7471
Maes Howe	Orkney	****	HY 3112
Unstan	Orkney	***	HY 2811
Wideford Hill	Orkney	***	HY 4012
Cuween Hill	Orkney	***	HY 3612
Taversoe Tuick	Orkney, Rousay	***	HY 4227
Blackhammer	Orkney, Rousay	***	HY 4127
Knowe of Yarso	Orkney, Rousay	***	HY 4028
Midhowe	Orkney, Rousay	****	HY 3730
Holm of Papa Westray	Orkney, Holm of Papa	****	HY 5051
Quoyness	Orkney, Sanday	***	HY 6737
Dwarfie Stane	Orkney, Hoy	****	HY 2400
Clach na Tiompan	Perthshire	***	NN 8333
Vementry	Shetland	***	HU 2961
Rudh' an Dunain	Skye	****	NG 3916
Mid Gleniron	Wigtownshire	**	NX 1861

Henges

Overhowden	Berwickshire	*	NT 4852
Balfarg	Fife	*	NO 2803

BRONZE-AGE REMAINS (2500 BC–700 BC)

Henges

Broomend of Crichie	Aberdeenshire	**	NJ 7719
Ballymeanoch	Argyll	**	NR 8396
Ring of Brodgar	Orkney	****	HY 2913
Stenness	Orkney	****	HY 3012
Muir of Ord	Ross & Cromarty	**	NH 5249
Cairnpapple	West Lothian	****	NS 9871

Stone Circles and Alignments

Ballymeanoch	Argyll	***	NR 8396
Achvanich	Caithness	**	ND 1841

SITE	COUNTY	RATING	GRID REF
Stone Circles and Alignments			
Hill o' Many Stanes	Caithness	★★	ND 2938
Upper Dounreay	Caithness	★	ND 0165
Whitecastles	Dumfriesshire	★	NY 2288
Lundin Links	Fife	★★★	NO 4002
Garynahine	Lewis	★★	NB 2330
Callanish	Lewis	★★★★	NB 2133
Croft Moraig	Perthshire	★★★	NN 7947
Torhouskie	Wigtownshire	★★★	NX 3856
Clava Cairns			
Clava	Inverness-shire	★★★★	NH 7544
Corrimony	Inverness-shire	★★★★	NH 3830
Recumbent Stone Circles			
East Aquhorthies	Aberdeenshire	★★★	NJ 7320
Loanhead	Aberdeenshire	★★★★	NJ 7428
Tomnaverie	Aberdeenshire	★★★	NJ 4803
Ring Cairns			
Sands of Forvie	Aberdeenshire	★	NK 0126
Old Keig	Aberdeenshire	★★	NJ 5919
Garrol Wood	Kincardineshire	★★	NO 7291
Round Cairns			
Memsie	Aberdeenshire	★★	NJ 9762
Kilmartin Glebe	Argyll	★★	NR 8398
Nether Largie	Argyll	★★★	NR 8398
Temple Wood	Argyll	★★★	NR 8297
Cup and Ring Stones			
Achnabreck	Argyll	★★★	NR 8590
Ballygowan	Argyll	★★	NR 8297
Baluachraig	Argyll	★★	NR 8397
Cairnbaan	Argyll	★	NR 8391
Kilmichael Glassary	Argyll	★★★	NR 8593
Big Balcraig	Wigtownshire	★★	NX 3744
Drumtroddan	Wigtownshire	★★★	NX 3644

IRON-AGE REMAINS (700 BC–AD 400)

SITE	COUNTY	RATING	GRID REF
Palisaded Sites			
Harehope	Peeblesshire	★★	NT 2044
Glenachan Rig	Peeblesshire	★	NT 1032
Shoulder Hill	Roxburghshire	★	NT 8223
Greenborough Hill	Roxburghshire	★	NT 8116
Forts			
(a) *Vitrified or Timber Laced*			
Abernethy	Angus	★★	NO 1815
Finavon	Angus	★★	NO 5055
White Caterthun	Angus	★★★★	NO 5466
Duntroon	Argyll	★★	NR 8095
The Knock	Ayrshire	★	NS 2026
Dunagoil	Bute	★★	NS 0853
Craig Phadrig	Inverness-shire	★★★	NH 6445
Burghead	Moray	★★★	NJ 1069
Dun of Relugas	Moray	★	NJ 0049
Dun Canna	Ross & Cromarty	★★	NC 1100
(b) *Forts with Untimbered Ramparts*			
Brown Caterthun	Angus	★★★★	NO 5566
Earn's Heugh	Berwickshire	★★	NT 8969
Garrywhin	Caithness	★★	ND 3141
Ben Freceadain	Caithness	★	ND 0555
Burnswark	Dumfriesshire	★★★	NY 1878
The Chesters, Drem	East Lothian	★★★	NT 5078
Traprain Law	East Lothian	★	NT 5874
Friar's Nose	East Lothian	★★	NT 6663
Norman's Law	Fife	★★	NO 3020
Denork	Fife	★★	NO 4513
The Moyle	Kirkcudbright	★	NX 8457
Arbory Hill	Lanarkshire	★★★	NS 9423
Braidwood	Midlothian	★★	NT 1959
Castle Law	Midlothian	★	NT 2263
Cademuir	Peeblesshire	★★	NT 2337
Whiteside Hill	Peeblesshire	★★★★	NT 1646

SITE	COUNTY	RATING	GRID REF
(b) *Forts with Untimbered Ramparts*			
Dreva Craig	Peeblesshire	★★★★	NT 1235
Walls Hill	Renfrewshire	★★	NS 4158
Eildon Hill	Roxburghshire	★★★	NT 5532
Hownam Rings	Roxburghshire	★★	NT 7919
Rubers Law	Roxburghshire	★★	NT 5815
Clickhimin	Shetland	★★★★	HU 4640
Ness of Burgi	Shetland	★★★	HU 3808

Brochs and Allied Structures

Bruan	Caithness	★	ND 3139
Keiss	Caithness	★★	ND 3561
Aikerness	Orkney, Mainland	★★★★	HY 3826
Glenelg	Inverness-shire	★★★★	NG 8217
Dun Carloway	Ross & Cromarty	★★★★	NB 1941
Caisteal Grugaig	Ross & Cromarty	★★★	NG 8625
Mousa	Shetland	★★★★	HU 4523
Clickhimin	Shetland	★★★★	HU 4640
Boreraig	Skye	★★★	NG 1953
Struanmore	Skye	★★★★	NG 3338
Torwood	Stirlingshire	★★	NS 8384
Dundornadilla	Sutherland	★★★★	NH 4544
Cinn Trolla	Sutherland	★★	NC 9290
Kilphedir	Sutherland	★	NC 9918
Dun Mor Vaul	Tiree	★★	NM 0449
Ardwell	Wigtownshire	★★	NX 0646

Crannogs

Milton Loch	Kirkcudbright	★	NX 8371

Souterrains

Ardestie	Angus	★★★	NO 5034
Carlungie	Angus	★★★	NO 5135
Crichton	Midlothian	★★	NT 4061
Castle Law	Midlothian	★★★	NT 2263
Grain	Orkney, Mainland	★★★	HY 4411
Rennibister	Orkney, Mainland	★★	HY 3912

SITE	COUNTY	RATING	GRID REF
Duns			
Ardifuar	Argyll	★★★	NR 7896
Druim an Duin	Argyll	★★	NR 7891
Kildonan	Argyll	★★★	NR 7827
Dun Grugaig	Inverness-shire	★★	NG 8515
Queen's View	Perthshire	★★	NN 8660
Balnacraig	Perthshire	★★★	NN 7447
Rudh an Dunain	Skye	★★	NG 3916

ROMAN REMAINS (*c* AD 75–200)

Antonine Wall			
New Kilpatrick Cemty	Dunbartonshire	★★★★	NS 5572
Callendar Park	Stirlingshire	★★	NS 8979
Watling Lodge	Stirlingshire	★★★	NS 8679
Tentfield Plantation	Stirlingshire	★★★★	NS 8579
Seabegs Wood	Stirlingshire	★★★★	NS 8179
Antonine Wall Forts			
Castlecary	Dunbartonshire	★	NS 7978
Rough Castle	Stirlingshire	★★★★	NS 8479
Other Forts			
Birrens	Dumfriesshire	★	NY 1878
Castle Greg	Midlothian	★★★★	NT 0459
Cramond	Midlothian	★★	NT 1977
Lyne	Peeblesshire	★★	NT 1840
Ardoch	Perthshire	★★★★	NN 8309
Inchtuthil	Perthshire	★★	NO 1239
Roman Siege Works			
Burnswark	Dumfriesshire	★★★	NY 1878
Woden Law	Roxburghshire	★★	NT 7612
Signal Stations			
Gask Ridge	Perthshire	★★	NN 9118–0220

DARK-AGE REMAINS (c AD 400–1200)

SITE	COUNTY	RATING	GRID REF
Forts			
Turin Hill	Angus	★★★	NO 5153
Dunadd	Argyll	★★★★	NR 8393
Kildonan	Argyll	★★	NR 2827
Dumbarton Rock	Dunbartonshire	★★	NS 4074
Dunearn	Fife	★★★	NT 2187
Craig Phadrig	Inverness-shire	★★	NH 6453
Trusty's Hill	Kirkcudbright	★★★	NX 5856
Mote of Mark	Kirkcudbright	★★	NX 8454
Dalmahoy	Midlothian	★★★	NT 1366
Burghead	Moray	★★★★	NJ 1069
Moncrieffe Hill	Perthshire	★★	NO 1320
Dundurn	Perthshire	★★★★	NN 7023
Dumyat	Stirlingshire	★★	NS 8397
Viking Sites			
Birsay	Orkney	★★★★	HY 2328
Orphir, Earl's Bu	Orkney	★	HY 3304
Jarlshof	Shetland	★★★★	HU 3909
Pictish Stones			
Dyce	Aberdeenshire	★	NJ 8813
Brandsbutt	Aberdeenshire	★★	NJ 7622
Maiden Stone	Aberdeenshire	★★	NJ 7024
Aberlemno	Angus	★★★★	NO 5255
Glamis Manse	Angus	★★★★	NO 3846
Eassie	Angus	★★★	NO 3547
Knocknagael	Inverness-shire	★★★	NH 6541
Fowlis Wester	Perthshire	★★	NN 9224
Abernethy	Perthshire	★★	NO 1916
Other Sculptured Stones			
Iona, St Martin's & St John's Crosses	Argyll	★★★★	NM 2824
Ruthwell Cross	Dumfriesshire	★★★★	NY 1068
Dogton Stone	Fife	★★	NT 2396

SITE	COUNTY	RATING	GRID REF
Kildalton	Islay	****	NR 4751
Barochan	Renfrewshire	**	NS 4069
Kirkmadrine	Wigtownshire	****	NX 0848
Monreith	Wigtownshire	**	NX 3542

MEDIEVAL REMAINS (AD 1000–1500)

Castles

(a) Mottes

Mote of Urr	Kirkcudbright	****	NX 8194
Coulter Motte	Lanarkshire	**	NT 0136
Hawick Motte	Roxburghshire	*	NT 5014

(b) Early Stone Castles

Peel of Lumphanan	Aberdeenshire	***	NJ 5703
Castle Sween	Argyll	***	NR 7178
Loch Doon	Ayrshire	**	NX 4895
Cubbie Roo's, Wyre	Orkney	**	HY 4426

(c) Curtain Wall Castles

Kildrummy Castle	Aberdeenshire	***	NJ 4516
Dunstaffnage Castle, Oban	Argyll	***	NM 8834
Rothesay Castle	Bute	***	NS 0864
Caerlaverock Castle	Dumfriesshire	****	NY 0265
Direlton Castle	East Lothian	****	NT 5183
Tantallon Castle	East Lothian	***	NT 5985
Bothwell Castle	Lanarkshire	****	NS 6859

(d) Tower Houses

Huntly	Aberdeenshire	****	NJ 5340
Affleck	Angus	**	NO 4938
Claypotts	Angus	****	NO 4531
Greenknowe, Gordon	Berwickshire	**	NT 6342
Castle Campbell	Clackmannan	***	NS 9699
Scotstarvit	Fife	**	NO 3711
Lochleven	Kinross	****	NO 1301
Threave	Kirkcudbright	****	NX 7362
Orchardton	Kirkcudbright	***	NX 8155

SITE	COUNTY	RATING	GRID REF
(d) *Tower Houses*			
Craignethan	Lanarkshire	★★★	NS 8146
Craigmillar	Midlothian	★★★★	NT 2871
Crichton	Midlothian	★★★	NT 3861
Hermitage	Roxburghshire	★★★★	NY 4996
(e) *Courtyard Castles*			
Tolquhon	Aberdeenshire	★★★	NJ 8728
Monastic Establishments			
Arbroath Abbey	Angus	★★	NO 6441
Crossraguel Abbey	Ayrshire	★★★	NS 2708
Dryburgh Abbey	Berwickshire	★★★★	NT 5931
Dunfermline Abbey	Fife	★	NT 0987
Inchcolm Abbey	Fife	★★★	NT 1982
Dundrennan Abbey	Kirkcudbright	★★	NX 7447
Sweetheart Abbey	Kirkcudbright	★★★★	NX 7362
Holyrood Abbey	Midlothian	★	NT 2673
Kelso Abbey	Roxburghshire	★★★	NT 7233
Jedburgh Abbey	Roxburghshire	★★★	NT 6520
Melrose Abbey	Roxburghshire	★★★★	NT 5434
Glenluce Abbey	Wigtownshire	★★★	NX 1856
Cathedrals			
St Machars, Aberdeen	Aberdeenshire	★★★★	NJ 9308
St Andrews	Fife	★★	NO 5116
Glasgow	Lanarkshire	★★★★	NS 6065
Elgin	Moray	★★★	NJ 2263
Kirkwall	Orkney	★★★★	HY 4410
Dunblane	Perthshire	★★★	NN 7801
Dunkeld	Perthshire	★★★★	NO 0242
Fortrose	Ross & Cromarty	★	NH 7256
Dornoch	Sutherland	★	NH 7989
Churches			
King's College, Aberdeen	Aberdeenshire	★★★★	NJ 9406
Fowlis Easter	Angus	★	NO 3233
Kilmory	Argyll	★	NR 7075
Lincluden	Dumfriesshire	★★★	NX 9977

SITE	COUNTY	RATING	GRID REF
St Mary's, Haddington	East Lothian	★★★	NT 5173
Seton Collegiate	East Lothian	★★★	NT 4175
Dunglass Collegiate	East Lothian	★★★	NT 7672
Aberdour	Fife	★★★	NT 1985
Leuchars	Fife	★★★★	NO 4521
Corstorphine	Midlothian	★★	NT 1973
St Giles, Edinburgh	Midlothian	★★★★	NT 2573
Roslin Chapel	Midlothian	★★★★	NT 2763
St Magnus, Egilsay	Orkney	★★★	HY 4630
Orphir, Mainland	Orkney	★★★	HY 3304
Grandtully	Perthshire	★	NN 8850
Muthill	Perthshire	★	NN 8617
Dalmeny	West Lothian	★★★	NT 1477
St Michael's, Linlithgow	West Lothian	★★★	NT 0077

Bridges

Brig-o-Doon	Ayrshire	★★	NS 3318
Dumfries	Dumfriesshire	★★★★	NX 9776
Cadger's Brig, Biggar	Lanarkshire	★	NT 0438

Villages

Kirkconnel, Waterbeck	Dumfriesshire	★★★	NY 2575
Dunrod	Dumfriesshire	★★	NX 6945
Galtway	Kirkcudbrightshire	★★★	NX 7048

POST-MEDIEVAL (*c* AD 1500–1850)

Palaces

Linlithgow	West Lothian	★★★★	NT 0077
Huntly Castle	Aberdeenshire	★★★	NJ 5340
Falkland Palace	Fife	★★★★	NO 2507
Edinburgh Castle	Midlothian	★★★★	NT 2573
Holyrood Palace	Midlothian	★★★★	NT 2673
Stirling Castle	Stirlingshire	★★★★	NS 7994

Artillery Forts

Ravenscraig Castle	Fife	★★★	NT 2992
Fort George	Inverness-shire	★★★★	NH 7656

SITE	COUNTY	RATING	GRID REF
Artillery Forts			
Ruthven Barracks	Inverness-shire	★★★	NN 7699
Craignethan Castle	Lanarkshire	★★★	NS 8146
Laird's Houses			
Glenbuchat Castle	Aberdeenshire	★★	NJ 3914
Castle of Park	Wigtownshire	★★	NX 1858
Stately Houses			
Inverary Castle	Argyll	★★★	NN 0908
Culzean Castle	Ayrshire	★★★	NS 2310
Traquair House	Peeblesshire	★★	NT 3334
Blair Castle	Perthshire	★★★	NN 8766
Hopetoun House	West Lothian	★★★★	NS 7909
Burghs with Fine Architecture			
Crail	Fife	★★★	NO 6108
Culross	Fife	★★★★	NS 9886
Stonehaven	Kincardineshire	★★	NO 8786
Edinburgh	Midlothian	★★★★	NT 2574
Elgin	Moray	★★	NJ 2162
Kirkwall	Orkney	★★★	HY 4511
Stirling	Stirlingshire	★★★	NS 7993
Particularly Fine Town Houses			
Provost Skene's House, Aberdeen	Aberdeenshire	★★★★	NJ 9305
The Palace, Culross	Fife	★★★★	NS 9885
Huntly House, Edinburgh	Midlothian	★★★★	NT 2673
Tankerness House, Kirkwall	Orkney	★★★★	HY 4410
Industrial Sites			
Bonawe	Argyll	★★★★	NN 0131
New Lanark	Lanarkshire	★★★★	NS 8842
Muirkirk	Ayrshire	★★	NS 6926
Wilsontown	Lanarkshire	★★	NS 9554

ACKNOWLEDGEMENTS

I should like to thank Miss Nancy Edwards who drew all the line illustrations, and also the following institutions for permission to reproduce photographs: The Scottish Tourist Board, Plates 1 (top), 7 (top), 10, 13 (bottom) and 16 (top); The National Trust for Scotland, 14; The National Museum of Antiquities of Scotland, 2 (top), 5 (top), 7 (bottom) and 12; The Department of the Environment (Crown Copyright Reserved), 2 (bottom), 4 (top and bottom), 9 (top and bottom), 13 (top) and 15; Aerofilms and Aero Pictorial Ltd, 3 (bottom).

INDEX